Praise for TO WALK IN INTEGRITY

A lovely meditation, brimming with wisdom and practical advice, on a skill in desperately short supply: authentic spiritual leadership. Steve Doughty eschews easy answers, instead offering graceful insights into time-honored virtues like simplicity, humility, compassion, and integrity. This book sets one afire with hope.

—PHILIP ZALESKI
Editor of *The Best American Spiritual Writing*

This helpful book acknowledges that contemporary culture is no friend of integrity. Doughty wisely recognizes there are no easy answers to this challenge and gently walks with his readers, raising insightful questions to create openings for maturing in integrity. His book contains practical leadership principles and inspires compassion and justice for a broken world.

—TOM SCHWANDA
Associate Professor of Spiritual Formation
Reformed Bible College
Grand Rapids, Michigan

Doughty writes with commendable clarity. His insights into the nature of integrity grow out of a biblical grounding and a theological perspective. Throughout the book he demonstrates what he is talking about by embodying his ideas in the lives and experiences of people.

—HARRY B. ADAMS
Horace Bushnell Professor Emeritus of Christian Nurture
Yale University Divinity School

In a meditative and practical way, using powerful illustrations, Doughty pursues the elusive meaning and understanding of integrity. Taking leadership far beyond issues of style, skill, and capability, he helps the reader identify and describe areas of truly integrated leadership behavior.

—THE REV. DR. JOHN D. SHARICK
Consultant to Congregations and Regional Church Bodies
Retired Presbytery Executive, Presbyterian Church (USA)

To Walk in Integrity is a heartfelt and moving testimony and guide to leadership with integrity. Doughty gently invites us into the company of those who have demonstrated such leadership. His book is a gift of love and a sign of hope for the church.

—JOHN BIERSDORF
Former President
Ecumenical Theological Seminary
Detroit, Michigan

To Walk in Integrity

SPIRITUAL LEADERSHIP IN TIMES OF CRISIS

STEVE DOUGHTY

UPPER ROOM BOOKS®
NASHVILLE

Cover design: Gore Studio, Inc. / www.GoreStudio.com
Cover photo: Jeremy Walker / The Image Bank
Interior design: Lori Lynch
Author photo: Joe Sherman / Photographic Artistry, Inc.
First printing: 2004

Library of Congress Cataloging-in-Publication Data
Doughty, Stephen V.
To walk in integrity : spiritual leadership in times of crisis / Steve Doughty.
    p. cm.
Includes bibliographical references.
ISBN 0-8358-9885-7
1. Christian leadership. 2. Spiritual life—Christianity. I. Title.
BV652.1.D68 2004
253—dc22

2004002628

Printed in the United States of America

For Jean

my best teacher and dearest friend

■ ■ ■

Contents

Acknowledgments

I AM DEEPLY GRATEFUL TO THE ENTIRE ASSEMBLAGE OF persons identified in the prologue. Far too numerous to mention by name, they have taught me through many years. When I was small, they pointed to a way of greater wholeness in life. As I grow older, they do not seem to quit.

I am indebted to Linda MacDonald, pastor of North Presbyterian Church, Kalamazoo, Michigan, and to all the people of that congregation, and also to pastors Kenneth Gill and Charles Shook of Longboat Island Chapel, Longboat Key, Florida. Together they show how wholly possible it is, and how needful, for persons in markedly different settings to walk in the way of integrity. I am grateful to friends who, through many patient conversations, have enriched my understanding of the subject this book seeks to explore: Fred Cunningham, Richard and Doris Strife, Delcy Kuhlman, Sister Elizabeth Smoyer, and Shirley Souder. I am profoundly thankful to JoAnn Miller, my editor at Upper Room Books, for her caring and wise counsel on the overall form of the book, and to Anne Trudel for her sensitive work in final preparation of the manuscript. I also wish to express my continuing gratitude to Upper Room staff members George Donigian, Jerry Haas, Tony Peterson, John Mogabgab, and Marjorie Thompson. Their ongoing encouragement has meant more to me than I can possibly tell them. I extend long-overdue thanks to my mentors Brevard Childs and Dick Sigler, whose counsel to search and to write has increasingly tugged at me. And most profoundly, I am grateful to my wife, Jean, for her wisdom, joy, and constant companionship through all seasons in this amazing gift of life.

Prologue

In Gratitude to a Strange and Steady Crew

THIS BOOK COMES FORTH WITH A LARGE MEASURE OF GRATI-tude to persons I have seen live faithfully through times of severe crisis. Some of these crises have been highly public. Others have been deeply personal, private, hidden from view. Yet whether a crisis has been open for all to see or known to only a few, under the most wrenching pressures these persons have held their center. With humility and absolute honesty they have remained true to God's leading in their lives. They have offered fresh vision in the midst of much pain.

As I reflect on these persons, I find they violate a major cultural norm. In a society that worships instant winners, their names do not always appear on the list of winners. Far from it. The just causes and needed struggles on which they so fully spend themselves often drag on rather than glide to swift triumph. The illnesses and family turmoils they contend with may pass but frequently do not. By current standards of quick resolution and ever-bright victory, their lives seldom measure up.

And yet if we watch these people with even a dash of thought-fulness, we realize our present system of measurement falls short, not their lives. Their very mode of being encompasses realms far broader and infinitely deeper than just the moment. Long after whatever they endured is over, the memory of these persons lingers in our minds, offering us life. Whatever may have been the outcome of the crisis they addressed, or even if no outcome is in sight, they beckon us, saying, "Look, for you too there is a way of faithfulness. In the midst of what you contend with right now, through all that may lie ahead, the way is here."

As I think about these individuals, I am grateful for an impression I cannot shake off: They are strange and they are steady. Both adjectives fit. The first one may seem an odd choice and hardly a compliment. Considered in its fullness, though, *strange* names an essential element in their way of being. *Strange* derives from the Latin word *extraneus*, meaning "foreign." In its earliest uses in the English language, *strange* meant "of another country." This is exactly the nature of the folk who live faithfully through crisis. They draw their values, customs, and deeds not from the swirling currents that press upon them but from another realm. In so doing they maintain their steadiness; they hold fast to their course. Though pressures may be great, they do not turn aside.

As I consider the strangeness and steadiness of these persons, I am ultimately grateful for where they point. With their presentation of something both good and alien in our midst, they direct us toward a way spoken of long ago by the psalmist who, in a season of much distress, still could say, "I have walked in my integrity" (Ps. 26:1). Those who point toward the way of integrity stretch and challenge us. At times they discomfort us. And the more I think on these persons, the more I am convinced that they offer the spiritual leadership we need in our troubled era. Wherever they find themselves right now, in whatever role they live out from day to day, they incarnate the wholeness we yearn for.

With gratitude, then, to those who point us in the right direction, I focus this book on walking in the way of integrity. It is obviously a small book. I cannot pretend to say all that could be said on the subject. Part of me senses that anyone attempting to write the definitive work on walking in integrity would eventually sigh and, with some sense of inner peace, fall utterly silent. That would be a good sign. The way of integrity will forever have more to reveal to us than we can say about it.

The movements of this book are simple. Part I provides a foundation. Chapter 1 considers the question, How shall we lead in times of crisis? It examines the breadth, strength, and depth of the question as we hear it today. Chapter 2 explores an ageless response to this question as offered in the biblical concept of walking in integrity. In Part II, chapters 3 through 11 examine qualities of persons who walk in integrity, and they explore how we ourselves might more fully walk in integrity. These meditative chapters have grown out of my own searching, and therefore I confess their incompleteness. I hope that all of these pages may stir the words that really matter: words among us, and words between us and the loving God whom we desire to serve in even the harshest places. To this end, each chapter provides two sets of questions at its conclusion, one for personal meditation and one for group reflection.

The need for spiritual leaders persists from age to age. Today's mounting crises make this need all the greater. I pray that we may learn from the strange, steady company that persists, sometimes against great odds, in offering healing for our human brokenness.

Part I

Spiritual Leadership, Crisis, and Integrity

Chapter 1

How Shall We Lead in Times of Crisis?

I RECENTLY ATTENDED A REGIONAL CHURCH MEETING THAT crystallized for many the importance of answering well the above question. Its two hundred participants comprised the usual steady crew for such events: pastors, educators, chaplains, and a host of conscientious lay leaders. On arriving, we tumbled out of cars, grateful to stretch our legs and happier still to see friends we had not glimpsed in months. We also silently lugged the usual baggage: anxiety over budgets, agitation flowing from never-ending conflicts, gnawing concern for sick parishioners and troubled families, uncertainties about the future of some program we cherished and knew others badly needed. Though I do not recall hearing anyone mention the matter amid all the glad "hellos," we also brought distress over an international situation that had run downhill for months.

After the opening prayer, we entered two markedly different experiences. The first, and longer lasting, came in the form of a carefully crafted praise service. Alleluias, bolstered by drums and acoustic guitars, bounced off the vaulted ceiling of the sanctuary. Two gifted, powerfully amplified sopranos encouraged us through the upward modulations of the hymns. In perfect time with the music, enormous images flashed on a screen that hung above the pulpit: smiling children, lush and rolling hillsides, brilliant light shining through trees. Even the most reserved among us couldn't resist tapping a toe now and then.

When the service ended, the chairperson invited us to approve the agenda for the meeting. We looked at it for thirty seconds and unanimously voted "Aye."

Then we started in a different direction. Initially we scarcely noticed the change. In accord with the agenda, a young woman from a developing nation came forward, bringing greetings from the churches of her land. She spoke softly, her presentation taking no more than the allotted seven minutes. She graciously gave thanks for the prayers she knew we offered for the churches she represented. Then she began to paint pictures for us with her words. Only now we no longer saw smiling faces, lush hillsides, and brilliant light shining through trees. We glimpsed weak-limbed bodies of the hungry, and forests destroyed to feed the engines of our country's economy. She became the first person that day to speak of the deteriorating international situation. Humbly but clearly she stated a belief lying at the core of the faith we shared. No one nation, no single ideology, no one way of life can proclaim itself the savior of the world; salvation comes from the One who has triumphed over death and persistently calls humankind to a new way of living.

With great gentleness she challenged us. We are, she said, called to be the body of Christ in the wealthiest and most powerful nation on earth. This comes as an immense and difficult calling. "I pray for you that by the grace of our loving God you may fulfill it." She encouraged us to face directly the crises surrounding us, both in our own country and in the world. She urged us to work for justice and to live prophetically for the sake of Jesus' healing love among all people. She asked that we continue to pray for the churches of her country because their calling also demands much, and less faithful, more soothing paths constantly tempt them. She concluded with an unforgettable smile. "May God guide you," she said, then returned to her seat.

I do not remember the next several items of business. Like many others, I lingered on the woman's words.

I do recall the observations of a fine old gentleman who sat next to me when the meeting broke for dinner. We had all, he said, entered devoutly into the worship service. Or, he qualified himself, probably as many persons as ever can become devout at any one time had done so. I nodded my agreement. And the people who planned and led the service had put their hearts, souls, and splendid gifts into every bit of it. I agreed again. And heaven knows—the fellow was getting warmed up now—we need to praise God for all the goodness we see, and we ought to do a darned lot better job of this than we have been! I nodded assent once more. "Yet," he said, looking me straight in the eye, "while all that wonderful praise touched the joys we brought to this meeting, it never acknowledged the pain. Not even the little hurts. And it never acknowledged the need to respond to the terrible pain in the world around us. Now take that young woman. What she said to us wasn't easy to listen to, but it was exactly what we needed to hear."

▪ ▪ ▪

How shall we lead in times of crisis? The young woman did not ask the question in our presence. Clearly, though, she had formed an answer. And because she lived that answer in our midst, she helped the rest of us look directly on terrible crises in our world. She caused us to hear Christ's relentless call to offer love and justice in the midst of these crises. And while she did not mention the host of local crises we bore in our minds that day, the authenticity of her presence reminded us of our need to acknowledge these other places of turmoil as well and to seek Christ in the midst of them.

How shall we lead in times of crisis? Whether we happen to be pastors or lay leaders, chaplains, educators, or administrators, we ask the question in a thousand different ways. It rides with us in the car as we hurry to hospitals. It clings to our backs as we enter difficult meetings. It thrashes about in our minds as we listen to the news and learn of events that will deeply shake the people we serve. How shall we provide the leadership of spirit that persons crave and we ourselves long for?

As we seek an answer, I believe that we would be wise to begin by taking time with the question itself. We need to sense its full dimensions. We need to grasp, as that young woman had obviously grasped, the vital, pressing force of the question in our current age.

The Breadth of the Question

In their provocative historical study *The Fourth Turning: An American Prophecy*, William Strauss and Neil Howe note that ever since the dawn of the modern era, Western culture has entered, on a cyclical basis, extended periods of crisis. Each period of crisis begins with a catalyst. Following the catalyst, other major distresses arise, including economic distress, distress over civil liberties, and an increase in domestic and international conflict. The most recent era of crisis, or "Fourth Turning" as the authors term such events, encompassed the Great Depression and the Second World War. Completing the book in 1997, Strauss and Howe predicted: "Sometime around the year 2005, perhaps a few years before or after, America will enter the Fourth Turning."[1] By any assessment, it appears that September 11, 2001, marks the entry into a new, extended era of crisis. And this present era, like its immediate predecessor, has swiftly swollen to global dimensions.

Crisis has laid hold on the human family through matters wholly independent of September 11, 2001. The HIV/AIDS epidemic continues to spread, creating great human suffering and destabilizing entire economies, particularly on the African continent. Recent estimates cite nearly fifteen thousand new infections each day, including children at the rate of one per minute.[2] How shall we lead in response to such human pain?

In 1992, 170 nations voluntarily agreed to reduce greenhouse gas emissions to 1990 levels. But during the following decade, carbon-based emissions increased globally by 9 percent and in the United States by 18 percent. Over three million people now die each year from the effects of air pollution.[3] Here too the word *crisis* fits. What healing leadership of spirit shall we offer? And as the worldwide list of such matters grows from one year to the next, the question itself finds ever-broader application.

Closer to home for many of us, state governments in the United States recently entered their worst economic crisis in over fifty years. Even the early phases of this crisis resulted in major cuts in funding for education and essential services to the elderly, the poor, and the mentally ill. Additionally, corporate mergers have continued to yield high profits for some and job loss for many. The disparity in income between the top 5 percent of society and the bottom 20 percent continues to grow.[4]

The question, How shall we lead in times of crisis? reaches to the very heart of life in the church. Internal conflict regularly surpasses critical levels. Theological differences within many church bodies, both Protestant and Catholic, slice chasms as wide as those that once existed between denominations. These divisions consume vast amounts of time and money. The church's mission of justice and redeeming love persists, but it has suffered. In spite of more than two decades of attention to mediation skills and conflict-resolution techniques, the frequency of major contention within congregations continues to mount, exacting a harsh toll from clergy and laity alike.

The future itself poses a crisis for the church, and this crisis takes diverse shapes. Who will provide pastoral leadership in twenty-five years? No, not twenty-five. Who will provide it in ten? Will we adapt to the new forms this leadership may take? What musical and other artistic expressions will embrace the fullness of faith and, at the same time, speak authentically to a culture that has radically changed? And what shape should the faith community itself take as it moves into the future? For centuries the parish church and vowed religious orders have offered the two main expressions of religious community. In many settings, both forms are severely pressed by social and economic change. To what fresh patterns of community might God be calling us? And if we catch the glimmer of an answer, will we dare begin to walk in its light?

> Naming where we see crisis can upset us. It probably ought to. Distress, at its best, creates awareness. It awakens us to where we are.

Crisis in the church presents itself in other forms. Burnout still consumes fine leaders. We earnestly seek to reclaim the gift of sabbath rest but institutionally and personally find it difficult, if not impossible, to abandon the drivenness of our days. An increasing number of persons who attend spiritual retreats describe themselves as "church alumni." Their presence attests that, to use John Milton's phrase from a similarly parched era nearly four centuries ago, somewhere along the way "The hungry Sheep look up, and are not fed."[5]

Naming where we see crisis today can, of course, upset us. Indeed, it probably ought to. Distress, at its best, creates awareness. It awakens us to where we are. And from our present discomfort, we can at least begin to catch a glimpse of the broad realms crying out for sustained spiritual leadership.

The Strength of the Question

How shall we lead in times of crisis? We begin to feel the strength of this question when we consider the meaning of the word *crisis*. To probe its meaning many persons have found it helpful to focus on the Chinese symbol for *crisis*. The symbol unites two characters: one stands for danger, the other for opportunity. These two words sum up the nature of many crises we encounter. Crises clearly offer peril. Just as clearly, they present opportunity. Even as a crisis threatens us, it can bring wholly unanticipated chances for personal and communal growth.

The Chinese symbol has enlarged our understanding of crisis. The only problem I have lies not at all with the symbol itself but with a nagging misuse of it. In United States culture there persists an all-too-prevalent tendency to accent the opportunity and downplay the danger. We say bravely, "Yes, the crisis is here!" Figuratively and literally adrenaline starts to flow. "Finally! Now we can act!" Then, our minds wedded to some gloriously positive outcome, we forge ahead, utterly oblivious to the more negative possibilities. If matters go awry, we are shocked.

The word *crisis* carries an added meaning that guards well against such evasion. In one of its most enduring uses in the English language, *crisis* applies to the critical phase in the progression of a disease. In medical terminology since the sixteenth century, a crisis has marked the decisive turning point. A crisis either results in fresh life and health for the patient or ends in death. To associate death with crisis sounds an exceedingly harsh note. It also, though, honors a long-standing usage of the word and takes with full seriousness the danger contained within the Chinese symbol.

The historic development of the word *crisis* provides further illumination. Our present word stems from the ancient Greek noun *krisis*, which built on the verb *krinein*, meaning "to separate, to distinguish, and to decide." The word *discern*, coming to us through the Latin, draws on this same Greek root. To be in crisis, then, is to be in a time of fundamental decision. It is to be at the point of forming a critical judgment. To be in crisis is to stand in the place of making an absolutely essential choice.

> To be in crisis is to be in a time of fundamental decision. It is to be at the point of forming a critical judgment.

What, then, does *crisis* mean? The word has grown too rich to admit a one-phrase definition. Its history stretches too far, its connotations extend too broadly for the word ever to slip into some slim envelope of understanding that anyone can open and instantly say, "Ah, that's it." Indeed, the very complexity of the word makes clear how vital a matter we deal with whenever crisis arises.

Crisis offers both great opportunity and searing danger. It carries the seeds of fresh life but also may end in death. Crisis calls forth, even demands, the deepest forms of discernment about how we shall live and act through the time of crisis. All this lends great potency to the question, How shall we lead in times of crisis?

The Depth of the Question

An elder in a parish I once served used to say, "We're having a season." Half the time he said it in the midst of jubilation, the other half in the midst of disaster. He never told us what kind of a season he meant, but he never needed to. After three horrible events, or sometimes only two, he would say with a shake of his head, "We're having a season." After two real joys (that was all it ever took), he issued the same pronouncement. Either way, the words always fit. I recall one year when, after a particularly extended series of tough situations, he declared, "These things don't know how to come in anything but seasons. They just can't stand being a single, lonesome storm."

The man was onto something about the way we experience crises, and his insight bears directly on the depth of the question, How can we lead in times of crisis? Like monsoon rains or winter blizzards, crises often come not singly but in series. The honest confession "I don't know if I can take any more" speaks this reality. Critical events can press on us one after another. We absorb the first, make crucial choices, try to adjust, then find ourselves in the same position all over again, and all over again after that.

My friend's concept of seasons fits where we find ourselves right now. Crisis comes upon us in the plural. When this happens, the question, How shall we lead? presses beyond issues treated in even the best of today's well-focused "how to" literature: how to deal with a shattering conflict; how to lead an organization through major change; how to speak, or simply be present, in the midst of a tragedy. We need all the guidance we can find on such matters. I shall forever be grateful to colleagues who, due to their wisdom, have again and again taught me how to deal more effectively with various tough situations. Yet if in a season of crisis I were to read all the books available on all the problems I could name, I still would not fully find what I need. In times of crisis, the whole shall always be greater than the sum of its parts. The plural itself, the living faithfully with one incident and another and then another, becomes an even larger issue. It undergirds and binds together all that we deal with.

How shall we lead in times of crisis? When we ask this question openly and fully aware that we live in an age of crisis, we become drawn to a new level of searching. We begin to wonder what pattern of living will yield a healing response even while much of what we contend with remains unresolved. How can we act in a way that will tender freshness of life, whatever may continue to happen? What mode of living will offer the steadiness that we and others yearn for? What way of carrying ourselves day to day will shine so brightly and speak so clearly that long after this harsh season is past, others will be able to look and say,

"There was a manner of living that told of wholeness then and beckons us even now"?

The question of how to lead in times of crisis reaches to every plane of our daily lives: our most public acts, our most private thoughts, our ongoing struggles. As we search out a response to the question, we can be sure that when we start to find it, the response itself will search us and shape us.

And it is toward this response that we now turn.

■ ■ ■

FOR PERSONAL MEDITATION

Reflect prayerfully on any of these questions as you find yourself led:

◆ When has another person directed my attention toward crises in the world around me? What enabled me to listen to that person? Or what turned me away?

◆ Where have I most experienced the press of crisis in my personal life?. . . in the life I share with others?. . . in the church? . . . in society and the world around me? Where do I most experience crisis now?

◆ Where have I seen crisis offer fresh opportunity? Where has it offered danger, even the need to discern between life and death?

◆ What have I learned in times of crisis? What has sustained me?

◆ What current crises exact from me the greatest toll? How am I called to grow in the face of these crises?

◆ In times of crisis, what do I most hope to offer back to others?

For Group Reflection

Explore together any of the following questions as you feel led:

◆ As we look over the preceding questions for personal meditation, do any particular insights or reflections come to us that we would like to share with one another? . . . to explore together?

◆ Where have we seen people deny the presence of crisis? Where have we ourselves wanted to deny its presence?

◆ In what particular crises right now do we see danger? . . . an opportunity to grow? . . . the need for deep discernment?

◆ What shapes do we currently see crisis taking in the world? . . . in the church? . . . in persons' lives?

◆ What do we feel we can most offer to the persons and groups that look to us for leadership in times of crisis? What more would we hope and pray that we might offer?

◆ As we close our time together, what crises do we wish to lift in prayer? For what insights do we offer thanksgiving?

Chapter 2

An Ageless Response:
Walk in Integrity

THE TELEPHONE RANG AS MOTHER AND I WERE FINISHING breakfast. My two oldest siblings lived several states away. Father had gone out the door for work twenty minutes before, followed by my older brother, who joined a car pool heading off to high school. Our aging cocker spaniel lay on the linoleum in front of the stove. The phone rang a second time. Nobody ever called at 7:15 AM. Mother left the table and picked up the receiver in the alcove where we stashed our winter boots and heavy jackets.

I chased the last of my Cheerios around the edge of the cereal bowl. "Oh dear," I heard Mother say. I caught the Cheerios. "Oh . . . oh dear," I heard her say again, and I could see her free hand twisting the phone cord. I stopped and waited. "Thank you so much for calling," she said. She hung up and walked back to the kitchen table.

The call did not relate to any of our family, although for the closeness of the person involved, it surely could have. "That was about Mr. Hales," Mother said, naming a longtime friend and then continuing with what she had just heard. Mr. Hales had become suddenly ill and was hospitalized in critical condition. Like my parents, he was less than fifty years old.

A short time later I boarded the bus for junior high. Throughout the day I thought of my parents' friend. His life had intertwined with ours for as long as I could remember. He had, I was sure, called me by name before I knew that name myself. I was certain he had done this with his ever-welcoming smile. Each year at Christmas our families gathered to sing carols. Not three months ago he and my parents had chaperoned a weekend excursion of high school students, and I had tagged along. There, as always, his warmth and gentle sense of humor set me at ease. I knew that he and my father had been friends since their late teens and had ventured into the business world just in time to catch the start of the Great Depression. Periodically, and with great respect, Father spoke of his friend's absolute honesty. I also knew what my parents once told me with admiration: Mr. Hales and his wife had, among their children, one born with severe mental handicaps. They had responded to the child's needs with wisdom in an age when there was less understanding of what to do than there is today. All these elements still pressed through my mind as I took the bus home that afternoon.

The next day a second telephone call came. That evening Mother and Father went over to be with Mr. Hales's widow. The day of the funeral, Father stayed home from work, and in the afternoon, while I was at school, he and Mother attended together.

As we sat at dinner that night, my parents shared a word I had not heard before but could not forget afterward. Never having gone to a funeral service, neither my brother nor I knew quite what to say or even what to ask, so we said little. Partway through the meal Mother brought up the matter herself. The service, she said, had been deeply helpful: the scriptures, the prayers, the gathering of a great many persons. "And," she added quietly, "the minister said our friend walked in his integrity."

My parents rarely missed a Sunday at church, but just as rarely did they quote the scriptures. To my relief they were not what people in our neck of the woods called "Bible thumpers." At this point, however, Mother went ahead and quoted the Bible anyway. "One of the psalm writers says, 'I have walked in my integrity.' Mr. Hales could have said that."

"What's integrity?" I asked.

"Integrity," my father answered. "Mr. Hales was integrity."

▤   ▤   ▤

THE DIFFERENT ELEMENTS OF THAT BRIEF CONVERSATION PLAYED about in my mind.

Integrity . . .

My parents' special friend . . .

The scripture . . .

What was this thing called integrity? One never works out such matters systematically. Not at first, anyway. If my parents' friend walked in integrity, then was his warmth the integrity? Was it the feeling of steadiness he seemed to convey no matter what was going on? Or was it something else? Was integrity somehow bound up with the wisdom he and his wife had shown as parents of a child with special needs? Was integrity what my father saw in this man's business dealings?

And there was the matter of the Bible. If the Bible mentioned integrity, then obviously this quality had been around for a long time. Integrity seemed to involve something deeper than, say, being a good member of the school board or of the League of Women Voters or even being a Democrat or a Republican.

In time the germ of an idea started to form. I realized that integrity embodied far more than just a single outward quality. Unlike someone's gait or laugh or tilt of the head, integrity permeated everything a person did. It was somehow a whole way of being. My parents accorded their friend a respect that they gave only to people they regarded as genuine leaders, so I knew integrity must be a characteristic of good leadership. In a deep family need and quite probably in dealing with the Great Depression, my parents' friend had met crisis with equanimity, so perhaps integrity offered a way of responding to various crises. And because integrity had been around for a long time, those who walked in integrity must live from something far broader than just the moment. The way of being to which these persons held appeared ageless. I groped for words to express all of this. I could not fully find them, but my sense of integrity's importance for our lives would not go away.

I still grope in my attempts to explain integrity. Perhaps we all do. Like the meaning of faith or the structure and beauty of a rose, integrity forever presents fresh unknowns. No matter how far we press toward understanding, we still have more to learn. Nevertheless, as with the perpetual marvels of nature and the riches of faith, our understanding of integrity can deepen. And as we press, we begin to see that the way of integrity extends a life-giving response to our search for spiritual leadership.

The Grounding of the Response

The way of integrity offers a ground for living as expansive as it is ageless. This ground poses a clear challenge to today's preoccupation with the self and self-fulfillment. It greatly stretches the more commonly accepted senses of what our lives are to be about. To see how fully this is so, it will be helpful to pause and look closely at the word *integrity* itself.[1]

Our current English word *integrity* carries the sense of two Latin words: *integer* and *integritas*. *Integer* meant "complete, whole, intact, pure." *Integritas* meant "unimpaired condition, soundness, uprightness, correctness." Today the word *integrity* conveys the meaning embraced by both these words: soundness, entirety, lack of corruption. To live with integrity is to be undivided. It is to stand complete and whole.

The scriptures encompass our present understanding of integrity and, at the same time, radically expand it. The Hebrew words for integrity are *tom* and *tummah*. Both derive from a verb meaning "to be complete." In the ample worldview of the Hebrews, however, human creatures can never attain completion on their own. Wholeness will come only in an ongoing relationship to Yahweh, the creator and source of all our being. Thus integrity embraces far more than just some fixed norm of moral behavior. Integrity cannot be reduced to a set of principles that a person may strive for and then check off as accomplished or well in hand. At its very core, integrity is grounded in a relationship to the living God whose wisdom, justice, and love shall forever exceed our own.[2]

> At its very core, integrity is grounded in a relationship to the living God.

The ancient Shema declares what breathes at the heart of integrity for the Hebrew people:

> Hear, O Israel: The LORD is our God, the LORD alone. You shall love the LORD your God with all your heart, and with all your soul, and with all your might.
>
> —DEUTERONOMY 6:4-5

The life of integrity holds God at the very center. It bends the heart, soul, and strength of life itself toward loving God. It grounds all deeds, all thoughts, all comings and goings in the divine-human bond.

The pages of the New Testament further enrich our understanding of integrity. Titus receives the admonition "in your teaching show integrity" (Titus 2:7). The Greek word for integrity here, *aphthoria*, carries connotations of "incorruptibility" and "soundness." It derives from the prefix *a*, meaning "away from," and the verb *phtheiro*, meaning "to corrupt." For Titus, to teach with integrity is not just to be moral and clear-headed. It is to be free from anything that will, either for himself or for his hearers, debase the bond with God.

Another New Testament term, *katharos*, lifts up the biblical vision of integrity. In its most literal sense, *katharos* means "pure," "clean." In its religious use, the word indicates ritual cleanliness and freedom from anything that will inhibit a relationship with God. To live with *katharos* is to desire to be faithful to God and God alone. "Blessed are the pure (*katharos*) in heart, for they will see God," says Jesus in the Sermon on the Mount (Matt. 5:8). Blessed are those who long to serve God in all things. So grounded, they shall indeed see God.

Nowhere in the scriptures can we find a hint that such grounding is easy. The tribes of Israel try it and stumble, try it and stumble, try it and stumble again. Even with the best of intentions, Jesus' disciples similarly go astray, and when they do get matters right, they frequently suffer rejection. Contrary to the proclamations of many popular forms of spirituality, grounding in the holy guarantees neither instant clarity nor instant success.

The above qualification noted, however, the fact remains that integrity finds its life in the ongoing bond with God and in holding this bond as the foundation for all else. Integrity does not draw its adherents into a deepening preoccupation with self. It points them toward life-stretching fidelity to the only One that can make us human creatures complete. Integrity is the Westminster divines proclaiming that the chief end of the human creature is "to glorify God, and to enjoy [God] forever."[3] Integrity is Ignatius of Loyola praying, "Lord, I freely yield all my freedom to you. Take my memory, my intellect, and my entire will. You have given me anything I am or have; I give it all back to you to stand under your will alone."[4] Integrity is our own yearning, in the midst of nearly impossible situations, to ally ourselves with God's yearning, even when we cannot precisely name that yearning. If we seek to live with integrity, the relationship with God becomes the ground from which all else grows. All deeds. All thoughts. Even all times of wondering and waiting.

The Cost of the Response

The way of integrity exacts a cost from those who follow it. Few phrases express this truth more succinctly than the declaration "Well, at least I kept my integrity." The speaker of these words has invariably suffered a loss—perhaps a job or public dignity or even health and cherished friends. He or she may also imply, "I held on to what I needed to. I kept the greater treasure." Even so, the sharp edges of privation have sliced deeply.

If we reflect on persons of integrity we have known, we can name some price that nearly each of them paid. A situation arose, and this person stepped forward. So, in all likelihood, did others. From our vantage point, they sacrificed greatly. We wonder how they did it. If we consider widely known figures of faith, we see that each paid dearly for acting with integrity. Moses. The Buddha. Muhammad. Esther. The prophets. Jesus on the cross. Each passed through some immense act of self-emptying. The same is true of more recent widely known leaders. Gandhi. Rosa Parks. Dorothy Day. Archbishop Oscar Romero. They fared no differently. At times the heavy side of "at least I kept my integrity" is exceedingly heavy.

The cost of integrity assumes a subtler form, less dramatic than outright sacrifice and loss but in its own way fully as demanding. Those who walk with integrity willingly pay the dues of constancy. We all know persons who become brilliant leaders in certain circumstances, but they lack what we would call integrity. By virtue of courage that rises to the moment, intellect, or sheer willpower, they exert great force. Their achievements in their area of influence may benefit many. The brilliance we see, though, is not constant. It has not moved into other parts of their lives. The lack that we find in them may sadden us. At times it may leave many others, and us, feeling deeply betrayed. This sense of betrayal may persist even if we continue to honor the goodness they offered.

Persons of integrity follow a different pattern. They do not maintain one set of values in public and another in private. They make no division between how they conduct themselves with those dearest to them and how they operate in other settings. When they act,

> Persons of integrity do not maintain one set of values in public and another in private. . . . They draw no distinction between major and minor moments.

they draw no distinction between major and minor moments. Each juncture in life, every chance meeting, every brief hour of activity pulses with equal value. They have chosen one ground for their lives and live from that ground wherever they find themselves.

With his familiar parable at the end of the Sermon on the Mount, Jesus points to the constancy practiced by those whose lives remain intact through even the harshest circumstances:

> Everyone then who hears these words of mine and acts on them will be like a wise man who built his house on rock. The rain fell, the floods came, and the winds blew and beat on that house, but it did not fall, because it had been founded on rock. And everyone who hears these words of mine and does not act on them will be like a foolish man who built his house on sand. The rain fell, and the floods came, and the winds blew and beat against that house, and it fell—and great was its fall!
>
> —MATTHEW 7:24-27

In Jesus' careful phrasing, the key to whether a life shall stand or fall lies not in the storm but in all that comes before it.

"Everyone then who hears these words of mine and acts on them" is the person whose life shall stand. So how has one lived day to day in accordance with Jesus' teachings? How, in circumstance after circumstance, has one responded to Jesus' invitation to a life of compassion and of communion with the living God? Has one remained attentive to the way of wholeness in all places? Jesus makes it plain: Any who seek wholeness in life willingly pay in the high coinage of constancy.

The Attraction of the Response

Ultimately the way of integrity attracts. Those who live it excite our interest in part because they do pay a cost. Their constancy and sacrifices demonstrate a wholeness of spirit. We discover in them what the masses found in Jesus: a congruity between words and deeds. The deeds of persons of integrity are wholly one with the fine words they speak.

The attraction deepens as we learn how fully we can trust such persons. We may not always like what they say, but we know they will be straight with us. They will not talk about us behind our backs or say one thing to us and something else to others. Persons of integrity may not have the most sparkling personality in the room or offer the most engaging conversation, but they possess a genuineness we can absolutely count on.

And because we trust such persons, we are particularly attracted to them in times of crisis. This does not mean they have all the answers. Indeed, at precisely the moment others offer facile solutions, these individuals may openly voice the wondering and distress the rest of us feel. They present us with no quick fix, no swift passage out of our current circumstances. Yet we sense that in their very way of being they are in touch with something far broader than just the moment. Their vision embraces wide horizons. Our crisis may be as personal as the search after a life-giving path for our days. It may be as broad as some tumult gripping all of society around us. Whatever the specific circumstance, persons of integrity draw us forth. Their way of being speaks of the wholeness we seek.

Real persons, grounded persons, persons willing to pay the cost—such individuals portray integrity. In drawing this portion of the book to a close, I would share just two such portrayals, one of them well-known, the other nearly hidden from view. Together they show the breadth of the way that beckons.

Writing from his cell in a Nazi prison camp, German pastor and theologian Dietrich Bonhoeffer asked, "Who stands his ground?" In the crisis of his day, who dared hold to a way different from the one dictated by an arrogance that threatened the world? Bonhoeffer surveyed the sources of support and guidance put forth by the culture surrounding him. Even the best he found wanting. In the end, he answered his own question:

> Who stands his ground? Only the man whose ultimate criterion is not in his reason, his principles, his conscience, his freedom or his virtue, but who is ready to sacrifice all these things when he is called to obedient and responsible action in faith and exclusive allegiance to God.[5]

For Bonhoeffer the only ground lay in the One who reached forth with constant cries for obedience and wholeness in the human family. Holding to this ground, Bonhoeffer paid with his life on a scaffold at Flossenbürg. He remains to this day an example of deep and healing fidelity in the midst of crisis.

I confess that a decade ago, the second example would not have crossed my mind. Now I find that those responsible for it stretch me on a weekly basis. For several years my wife and I have worshiped with a small, urban congregation, nearly half of whose members live with chronic mental illness. Their conditions include schizophrenia, bipolar disorder, accident-induced brain damage, and a long list of other afflictions they never sought and the best of medical science cannot remove. On any given Sunday, some come shining with joy and others bearing pain that goes deeper than anything the two of us have ever known. With disarming openness, they offer their prayers. They give thanks for the most basic gifts: a job, new glasses, a birthday, friendship. They intercede for troubled friends, warring nations, injured roommates, and ailing parents. As supplicants, they earnestly pray for the ability to forgive those who don't understand them and for grace to live steadfastly through another week.

I don't mean to romanticize these persons. They struggle to be faithful as much as anyone else. Their gift to us, though, is plain. With undiluted clarity they know their chosen ground. They seek this ground, and they know that the One who is their ground steadily seeks them. If my wife and I were to receive a triple measure of God's grace, I doubt that we would ever match the strength of spiritual leadership these persons show.

We pass through many crises in our lives. Some of these are global, some intimate, some both. We long to live faithfully through such crises when they come. And just as much, we long to live in a manner that will help others find wholeness, even when crises come one upon another, even when the most difficult situations persist from year to year and much remains unresolved. Though the way of integrity asks much, clearly it comes forth as a life-shaping response to our longing.

■ ■ ■

FOR PERSONAL MEDITATION

◆ Who, early in my life, showed me what it means to walk with integrity? What attracted me to this person? For what now do I give thanks as I meditate on this person?

◆ What different grounds have I chosen for my life through the years? What have they yielded? What have I learned?

◆ Persons of integrity "draw no distinction between major and minor moments." What are some "minor moments," when the integrity of another became vitally important to me? And when, even in little things, has it become important to me to maintain my integrity?

◆ When have I feared the cost of integrity? When have I been willing to pay it?

◆ What situations challenge me to live with integrity right now?

FOR GROUP REFLECTION

Explore together any of the following areas:

◆ What particular thoughts came to us as we considered the above questions?

◆ As we reflect on persons of integrity, what questions would we most like to ask them? How do we think they might respond?

◆ "Grounding in the holy guarantees neither instant clarity nor instant success." What do we think of this statement? What would we add to it? Where have we seen persons forgo instant clarity and instant success in order to remain grounded in the holy?

◆ This chapter observed, "The deeds of persons of integrity are wholly one with the fine words they speak." When people look at the church, where do they see integrity? Where do they fail to see it? What might we do, gently or perhaps not so gently, to encourage the church to grow in integrity?

♦ For what areas shall we pray in our own lives, and for what areas shall we pray in the life of the church, that we willingly pay the cost of integrity?

Part II

Integrity Lived:
Signs and Openings

WHAT EXACTLY DOES IT MEAN TO WALK IN INTEGRITY? How can we more fully walk in the way of integrity ourselves?

These questions admit no simple answers. I doubt that I shall ever see an article or a book titled *Ten Easy Steps to Integrity*. And if I do, I confess that it will make me awfully nervous. Those who live with integrity go about the steady business of rooting their lives in the One who reaches toward us all. Their lives appear far too demanding and too much of a whole to be fractured into a series of easily imitated steps.

What I do see as I watch those who live with integrity are subtle signs pointing to the way of integrity. The signs quietly say, "Yes, here is integrity" and "Here it is again." They also point to those who walk in integrity, indicating, "Here lives another person traversing this good and demanding way."

As I look closely at these signs, I realize that they are also openings. For those considering the nature of integrity, they provide entrance to a fuller understanding of what integrity is about. And for those seeking to walk with integrity, they become passageways for further immersion in the way of integrity.

Movement among these signs and openings is primarily a movement of ever-greater immersion in the way of integrity rather than linear progression from one particular point to another. Those who walk in integrity may for a time attend more to one portion of the way than to others, but ultimately they enter more deeply into all that spreads before them.

The following chapters provide a series of meditations on the signs and openings of integrity. Like all meditations, not one is complete. Each invites the reader to prayerful reflection and wider exploration.

We live in an age that desperately needs the faithful witness of persons walking in the way of integrity. I am convinced that as we reflect together we shall come to see this ageless way more clearly. And if we so desire, by the grace of the God who yearns to make us whole, we shall venture more fully into this way wherever we may find ourselves.

Chapter 3

Mystery

The older I get, the less I know.
—AN OLD PRESBYTERIAN FARMER

THE MAN WHO SPOKE THE ABOVE WORDS SAID THEM WITH
a glint in his eyes. He was talking to my wife while his son milked
the cows. As for my referring to him as old, I don't think he'd mind
a bit. "That's exactly what I was," he'd say in his gravelly voice. As
for "Presbyterian," he was that too; and I use the word not because
he was of my own denomination and a member of the first parish
I served, but because he was a devout man and "Presbyterian" happened to be his way of expressing that devotion. As for his knowing less and less the older he got, my wife smiled when she told me
late that afternoon. He must have been over eighty, and we, just
cracking thirty and supremely sure of ourselves, had quite a ways
to go. We have cherished his wisdom ever since.

The farmer's observation came back to me with particular
strength one morning a couple of years ago. I received a Christmas
letter from a Roman Catholic priest who had participated in a
monthly prayer group I attended before he moved a thousand miles
out west to serve a new position in his order. He wrote simply,

43

"God has allowed me to continue in the ministry of spiritual direction out here. The more I'm involved, the more I know how deeply I do not know."

When I reflect on these two incidents, I am caught by the glint in the eyes of the farmer and the word *deeply* as used by the priest. The farmer, it appeared, had relaxed into his state of not fully knowing—he had more than relaxed, actually. Clearly he delighted in this state as he watched his son labor away and reported his discovery to my wife. As for the priest's use of *deeply*, he was a thoughtful person and employed words carefully. He might have written, "The more I'm involved, the more I know how *much* I do not know." That would have implied a concern for quantity, for some expanse of knowledge still to be mastered. Quantity, though, lay far from this man's mind. *Deeply* pointed to his own inner state. Coming from him, the word expressed an increasing wonder. The further he went into the call God had granted him, the greater his wonder became. I did not see his face as he wrote the word, but knowing him, I could sense a wide-eyed marveling. On some sacred level the priest and the old Presbyterian farmer were one.

Mystery, that which we cannot fully know, lies at the heart of faith-filled experience. "Mystery," writes psychiatrist Harvey Rich, "is different from the 'yet-to-be-discovered.'"[1] Mystery is not a new page of knowledge we eventually turn over, read, and understand, thus causing the mystery to vanish. Instead, mystery is a page we open, and suddenly we find ourselves drawn into the words, the print, the very fabric of the paper. We realize we have entered not just one more page of life but an immensity we will never completely comprehend because somehow that immensity comprehends us and stretches toward an infinity we cannot fully see.

Mystery ever approaches us in the particular. A long line of geese arcs northward across the salmon sky of a late March afternoon, drawing us upward into their flight. Stars stop us in our tracks on a cold winter night. In a subway car bursting from the crush of its passengers, a young mother smiles at her sleeping infant, and an older woman, smiling herself, holds at least as tightly to the young mother's smile as she does to the pole that braces her against the lurching of the car. One Saturday evening I cup in my hands a small, gray rock my wife has just given me. It has come, she tells me, from the shores of Lake Michigan. And because of where it comes from, I start to hear laughter from long ago and my mother's voice. I see gulls glide swiftly over the water, feel cool waves lick about my waist, and am overcome with a wholeness I cannot put into words.

"What people yearn for today," said a pastor over lunch, "is not information but connection." He named both a major hunger of our age and the direction in which mystery ultimately takes us. We do not need more data in our lives. We need

> Those who walk in integrity bow before the mystery. They allow themselves to be seized by what meets them in the mystery.

to find our place again, to rediscover our bonds. Amid the lethal fractures of our world, we long to uncover and affirm the greater depths of being wherein we all are one. And it is precisely into these greater depths that divine mystery draws us. In these depths we fall silent because, through what we have seen or heard or felt touch our flesh, we know that a graced Immensity reaches toward us and binds us all. Out of these life-giving depths we hear: "This is my body. This is my blood. Partake of it, all of you." While immersed in these depths, a man many judged to be half-mad wrote to a fiercely divided society, "There is one body and one Spirit, just as you were called to the one hope of your calling, one Lord, one faith, one baptism, one God and Father of all, who is above all and through all and in all" (Eph. 4:4-6). What meets us in the heart of mystery presses to unite us. It actively seeks to make us one.

Mystery serves as the foundation of our growth toward wholeness. Both personally and corporately, our movement toward completion starts with our being overwhelmed by a reality we shall never fully be able to name. "Religions begin as a salve to mystery, not a manifesto of truth," writes Terry Tempest Williams.[2] Sound teachings can interpret our experiences. Wise words can guide us. Mystery, however, remains the site of beginnings. And those who truly walk in integrity model a way of being that lives close to the mystery. More precisely, they bow before the mystery, and then they allow themselves to be seized by what meets them in the mystery.

To Bow

In the scriptures, at times persons bow before mystery in the most literal sense. Stunned by what he sees in Jesus, Peter throws himself down at Jesus' knees (Luke 5:1-8). Less impetuously, perhaps, but just as intensely, a woman cured of a twelve-year hemorrhage falls trembling before the Galilean whose garment she has just touched (Mark 5:25-34).

More often persons bow figuratively. In broad lines an ancient psalmist sings:

> The heavens are telling the glory of God;
>> and the firmament proclaims his handiwork.
> Day to day pours forth speech,
>> and night to night declares knowledge.
> There is no speech, nor are there words;
>> their voice is not heard;
> yet their voice goes out through all the earth,
>> and their words to the end of the world.
>> —PSALM 19:1-4

The Bible gives us no image of the author of these words. We see no arms stretched forth, no figure prostrate on the ground. Still we sense the full bending of the person, the marvel-filled mind, the amazed spirit, the life stopped in its tracks and staring in wonder. This is like the bowing of Mary as she is struck dumb at the moment of the Annunciation (Luke 1:26-38), barely able to gasp, "How can this be?" It is like the bowing of Moses in the presence of a burning bush (Exod. 3:1-6), lurching away from his chosen path, stumbling headlong over brush and boulders to see what on earth is happening with this unimaginable sight.

To bow before the mystery means stopping in one's tracks, turning aside, staring in wonder. And such bowing seems nearly impossible in our culture and in the church today.

I have few regrets about the years I spent serving in what can properly be called my denomination's ecclesiastical bureaucracy. I have always believed my time in that realm was in response to a genuine call. Much that I saw from my role moved me. Both regionally and nationally I worked with as devoted a body of persons as I have ever known. At the same time, I witnessed a mystery-suffocating haste that increasingly grieved me and many of my colleagues. This haste was the product of no one person but persisted as "part of the system," and of course we all were part of the system in our denomination. Our denominational system, it appears, was part of a far larger societal system, and rail as we might against the situation, matters seldom changed.

This mystery-suffocating haste manifested itself in a multitude of ways and continues to do so. A theologian gives a splendid address to some three hundred church leaders from across the country. Her words are full of prayer, her insights deep. We quietly pull away from our laptops and set down our pens, seeking to absorb her message. But as soon as she finishes, we cluster into buzzing little groups and in forty-five minutes hack out Six Action Steps in response to what we have just heard. Then, after a break for refreshments, we hurriedly gather about some completely different topic. Once ("and I'm not making this up") I belonged to a regional church body that identified its Eight Most Urgent Concerns. A few items got left off the list, so the next year we identified our Seven Additional Most Urgent Concerns. At that point we had Fifteen Most Urgent Concerns.

Consider what takes place at regional and national meetings of religious groups, regardless of whether they are Protestant, Catholic, nondenominational, or interdenominational. We start working together at 8:30 AM, break for lunch, go back to work, break but do not really stop for dinner, and plan to continue until 9:00 PM but then extend the hour. We continue this pace day after day, meeting after meeting, in spite of nearly universal agreement that "this is not healthy." "We are trying to do far too much." "There must be a better way."

The above instances mirror both the grander and the more intimate scheme of things. In the widest expanse of society and in the innermost places of our hearts, we feel the pressure, the cascading rush, and ultimately, accompanying these, a gnawing lack of fulfillment. We feel such emotions unless, of course, we employ business to distract us from our deeper wondering. And in the end, even when we try to avoid the matter, a single line of questioning asserts itself. Where in our present pattern of living do we find space for the divine mystery to breathe fresh life upon us? Where among us lives the humility to stop dead in our tracks and let go of our desire to control every step and plan every detail? Where stands the will to attend wholly on the stunning wisdom we have just heard from the mouth of another or on the Voice we have heard cry out from a single Most Urgent Concern?

I must confess that in all of these situations I have been given some moments of hope. I don't want to overstate their presence, but it would be an act of faithlessness to ignore them. I think of a church leader I observed on a three-day group retreat a few years ago. He said not one word the whole time. He simply listened. He did this neither to seem empathetic to the many in attendance who knew him nor to gain information for his complex, often difficult role in the church. As the days passed, his eyes gave away his purpose. He was delighting in the sacredness of each life around him.

I think of the increasing number of persons I have encountered in recent years who seek times of silence. Silence in their personal lives. Silence in corporate worship. And not only silence in these more common realms but also silence in meetings and group deliberations. Silence for listening for the movement of the Holy Spirit. Silence that opens to God's presence in the midst of searing pain, fierce anger, sudden wonder, and spontaneous joy.

I think of the fifteen lay leaders and two pastors on a church board who faced an immensely divisive situation. They invited me to attend their monthly meeting in case they needed a referee. Not once that night did they call on me, but I will forever be grateful for what they showed me. They began their meeting as they always did, with prayer and time for one of their number to offer her faith journey. The woman whose turn it was talked for forty-five minutes. Nobody fidgeted or checked a watch. The entire group hung on every word, every struggle, every honest and agonizing question, and every affirmation. They were in the presence of something holy, and they knew it. In the fullest sense of the word, they bowed. After the woman finished, the group prayed again. Over the next forty-five minutes, with great honesty, they dealt with the divisive issue. When they finished that evening, they did not all agree, but they had come together on a level deeper than their differences and more enduring than anything their outside referee might have fashioned.

> Faith demands that we recover the good sense to stop, bow before wonders, and let the divine mystery breathe forth again in our midst.

Such incidents serve as a reminder. If we are to grow rich in the life of the Spirit, we must first open to what God is actually doing among us. In this driven age, faith does not require that we pack still more items into a meeting agenda or stuff more activities into our already overcrowded days. Faith demands that we recover the good sense to stop, bow before beckoning wonders, and let the divine mystery breathe forth again in our midst.

To Be Seized

To bow before mystery, to honor it in our public and private worlds, only begins the journey. Those who walk in the way of wholeness show us more. Peter does not stay forever prostrate before Jesus. He gets up and joins the One who has called him through the mystery (Luke 5:11). He will spend the rest of his days discovering the meaning of this summons, but he follows. The writer of Psalm 19 does not stay frozen, gazing up at the stars, but bends every ounce of skillful craft to tell all generations what blazes from the skies.

Moses spends forty years answering the Voice that spoke out of the bush. Over all that time he struggles and stammers; becomes angry, disappointed, and exhausted; and knows he won't even get to complete the project. Mary, after the angel's flood of eloquent words, simply responds, "Let it be with me according to your word" (Luke 1:38). Forty days after Jesus' birth she hears, "a sword will pierce your own soul too" (Luke 2:35). This pronouncement does nothing to alter her initial assent.

On whatever level we choose to deal with such accounts, the biblical literature remains constant in its treatment of mystery. Nowhere does the Bible romanticize mystery or exalt religious experience for its own sake. What remains central in each instance is the response of the person to what beckons through the mystery. And the essence of faithful response is the willingness to be drawn forth completely by what calls from the heart of the mystery. What matters supremely is the "yes," the letting go, the yielding to a whole new way. In the words of psychiatrist Gerald May, "It is not for us to use the power of mystery, but for us to be used by it. We do not embrace it in our arms, it embraces us. We do not capture it but are captured by it."[3]

Those who walk in the way of integrity become the willingly captured, the assentingly seized. They are Julian of Norwich and Teresa of Ávila pouring forth new images of the divine, not because the old images were wrong but because they have been seized by a reality too great for any one image to contain. The assentingly seized include modern-day theologians and honest faith searchers doing the same. The assentingly seized include two persons dear to me who live in response to what one calls the Paschal Mystery. By that she means the mystery incarnate at Easter, the mystery of new life greening forth in the midst of death. For one of these two, responding to the Paschal Mystery means steadily intertwining her life and her abundant creativity with persons who will never set foot outside the walls of a federal prison. The other sits in homes, hospitals, and hospice care centers holding the hands of the dying.

Ultimately the willingness to be seized by mystery allows such persons to mark a fresh way in our world. Amid all the craziness and conflicts and crises, they become tellers of the holy. They speak with their lives. With their deeds and their very way of being, they portray a way of wholeness that beckons us all.

■　■　■

FOR PERSONAL MEDITATION

♦ When have I felt the presence of mystery coming to me through contact with another person? . . . or in nature? . . . or in a cry of pain? . . . or in some other way?

♦ How have I bowed before mystery? And how have I turned away?

◆ As I reflect on experiences of mystery in my life, for what do I give thanks? And what would I seek so that I may respond more fully to mystery?

◆ As a leader, am I patterning my life in such a way as to encourage others also to respond to mystery?

FOR GROUP REFLECTION

◆ Where have we experienced "mystery-suffocating haste" in our own lives? . . . in the religious community? . . . in the culture around us?

◆ What hopeful, helpful steps have we seen others take to allow room for mystery? What steps have we ourselves taken, or what steps might we take? What steps might our own group take to encourage a greater openness to mystery in the wider organization(s) of which we are a part?

◆ What steps does the church as a whole need to take to allow for greater openness to mystery? . . . to allow for fuller response to mystery?

◆ The chapter notes, "What meets us in the heart of mystery presses to unite us." Where have we seen an awareness of mystery break down barriers between people and draw them into unity? Where do we pray that this might happen now?

Chapter 4

Humility

THOSE WHO WALK IN INTEGRITY ACT WITH HUMILITY. IN THE midst of crisis, the completeness that speaks through their lives sounds a very different tone in our world than the arrogant boast, the power-asserting threat, and the proud claim to absolute righteousness.

We have grown all too familiar in our age with the assertion "I have it." This assertion resounds on both the national and international scene. It finds expression in the church and even in the most intimate of personal bonds. The assertion may come loud and strong: "I have the positional power, so you need to pay attention." "We possess the armies and the wealth." "My side holds the truth." The assertion may be as silent as a glance, as subtle and sharp as the turn of a put-down phrase. Or rather than exert any outward pressure or threat, the "I have it" may allure. It may entice with lavish promises.

In whatever form it comes, the "I have it" assertion commands authority. People respond. Cowed, genuinely excited, or simply relieved at being handed a quick solution to frightening problems, persons follow. Ranks expand, as do hopes. However, even where excitement mounts and triumph appears imminent, in the end followers often feel they were seduced rather than led. Hope fades into disillusionment. The "I have it" assertion may gain ascent for a time, but finally and at best, it falls flat. Often it breeds deep division. At worst, it destroys many. The sad histories of war, racial conflict, and religious strife speak its dangers only too well.

> To act with humility is in no way to cower or to hold back.

Whether we encounter the "I have it" assertion in another's easy confidence or in our own swelling self-assurance, we may at first experience discomfort. We may say inwardly, "This does not quite ring true" or "What I am feeling here does not seem right." We may sense we are being pulled by something less than genuine. We may, for at least a moment, perceive that what attracts us is not whole and will never lead to wholeness in the human family. Still, the "I have it" both presses and tugs. It does so with particular effectiveness in times of turbulence and change, when the desire for absolute certainty runs strong.

Humility, on the other hand, offers something quite different. The humble claim for themselves no absolute authority. They pretend no perfect wisdom. The word *humility* derives from the Latin *humus*, meaning "ground" and "earth." Those acting with humility do not sound the note "I have it." Their song begins, "I am of the dust." In the midst of both crisis and calm their manner of carrying themselves proclaims, "I am finite. I do not possess all knowledge, all strength, all skill, and I never shall." Whether or not they have read deeply in the scriptures, they know in their hearts the wisdom found there. They have grasped that only through humility shall they begin to find true exaltation (2 Sam. 22:28; Prov. 29:23). Only with humility as a primary element in their deeds will they move toward the wholeness they seek (Eph. 4:1-3).

To act with humility is in no way to cower or to hold back. Indeed, when it comes to acting on difficult issues, the humble often become the boldest. Knowing their limitations, they stand free of any need to pretend to be more than they are. Knowing their finite place in relation to the One who reaches toward all, they open to God and others in a way that pride will never allow. They offer a form of leadership that springs from roots wholly different from those that feed "I have it." Their leadership is fresh and life-giving. To see how completely this is so, it will be helpful here to look more closely at humility and at three particular components that weave steadily throughout the deeds of the humble: repentance, dependence, and openness.

Repentance

Repentance is hardly a popular practice. It never really has been, but its level of disfavor today appears to be approaching an all-time high. Mere mention of the word conjures up a spate of unfavorable images: the scowling face, the shaking fist, the mouth wide open and hurling the single, angry imperative "Repent!" Any church that offers "A Brand New Course on Repentance" will hardly draw in persons from the street or even away from the ragged edges of its coffee hour. The chief bond between repentance and sin today inheres far less in matters of theology than in a pervading sense of "Gosh. Do we really have to deal with this sort of thing anymore?"

The problem with the rejection of repentance is twofold. First, repentance appears to be anything but a side issue in genuine spiritual formation. In the Gospel of Matthew, when Jesus begins to preach, "Repent" is the first word out of his mouth (4:17). In Mark, before Jesus even gets started, John the Baptist commands repentance as an absolute precondition for opening to the reign of God (1:4). In the Hebrew scriptures, the prophets endlessly

call on the people to repent. Among the most moving passages
in the book of Psalms is an unfettered penitential cry:

> Have mercy on me, O God,
>   according to your steadfast love;
> according to your abundant mercy
>   blot out my transgressions.
> Wash me thoroughly from my iniquity,
>   and cleanse me from my sin.
>
> For I know my transgressions,
>   and my sin is ever before me.
>
> —PSALM 51:1-3

Ultimately the biblical understanding of repentance is not at
all about the scowling face, the shaking fist, and the angry demand. It is about turning from what does not work in life to
what does. And herein lies the second problem with today's rejection of repentance: It scraps a stereotype that ought to be set
aside but then fails to embrace the reality of our human brokenness and our desperate need to move beyond all that con-
tributes to this brokenness.

I cannot fully visualize the Jesus of Matthew's Gospel deliver-
ing his early messages. Nor can I catch the precise sound of John
the Baptist preaching beyond the Jordan. What I clearly sense,
though, is that Jesus and John never slipped into the ego-bloated
"I have it" form of preaching that many in our age have rightly rejected. Their vision of human need was too broad for that, their
understanding of repentance too deep. The cry "Repent" came
from their lips for the same reason it came from the mouths of the
prophets and for the same reason "Have mercy on me, O God"
rang out from the soul of the psalmist. They saw the brokenness of
the human condition; in pointing to repentance, they named the
need to turn from all that would perpetuate this brokenness.

Those who walk with integrity heed the call to repentance. Their longing for wholeness will not let them do anything else. They know their own weaknesses. They understand that even if they have committed themselves to an upright life, the old capacities for lust, greed, sloth, and pride remain. Their honest humility is in no small part born of knowing that they, like all others, have fallen short of the glory of God and, no doubt, will continue to do so. They have had to let go of much in their lives that has pulled them down. They know they will need to go on doing so.

Humility that grows from genuine repentance sets free rather than debilitates. It liberates from self-righteousness and the barriers self-righteousness invariably erects. It allows a person to say from the heart, "I am truly sorry for what I did." It enables one to look within and say, "Yes, I too have all these other ways I need to keep growing."

Humility that grows from genuine repentance also allows for courageous connection with the world's wider wounds. I have long cherished a story that a college friend shared with me. He had learned it from his father. Even when my friend told me, our world differed substantially from that in which the incident occurred, but the event itself was too daring and too much needed to be confined to any one age.

On the day Germany surrendered in World War II, a large celebration broke out in the small midwestern town where my friend's father lived. That night persons from all over the region packed into the stone church at the center of town. They smiled, laughed, and called out in joy. The minister, a soft-spoken man, stood before them. To the congregation's astonishment, he asked them to get down on their knees and ask forgiveness for what had gone on during the preceding years. His invitation contained nothing overbearing or lordly, not a hint of superiority. Certainly it held nothing against the young adults of that community who had gone into battle, young adults he had prayed for daily, young adults whose families he sought to comfort when they had died. The minister issued the invitation just once. Then he stepped away from the pulpit and knelt. Not for effect or for show. He simply felt the brokenness, the need to ask mercy, the inner imperative to turn to a better way.

Some in the congregation grew angry. Some just gaped. Bit by bit, many knelt. My friend's father joined them. He never forgot the moment, nor has my friend. Nor have I, though I never met the minister and have not once stepped inside that church.

Dependence

The humility of those who dare to lead us in fresh ways grows also from dependence. In the midst of crises, the underlying message of their lives is, "Not of myself am I able to do what I am doing." Whether they speak boldly, confess the need to find a better way, or simply endure in a manner that offers signs of healing, their actions remain unpretentious. From deep within they convey the constant, trusting sense, "I am able to act now only by the goodness of the One who reaches toward us all."

In varied forms, dependence comes forth as a universal theme of religious faiths. Whether the worshiper cries out to Yahweh, Abba, or Allah, the source of daily guidance and sustenance lies not in the self but beyond. Whether one seeks to grow in the wisdom of the Tao or in the lavish inventiveness of the native people's Creator, the riches of life are too immeasurably vast for us to attain on our own. The steps we take, we are not meant to take alone. We are to lean. We are to rely on that which dwells in mystery and yet remains as immediate as the next five minutes of our lives.

Artists, teachers, and parents know this pattern of humble dependence even when they do not name it. So do health care providers, public safety officers, and any others regularly stretched beyond their own finite abilities. "Every time I sing in front of a group," a fine musician said as we shared tea one morning, "I pray before I get up. I just say, 'Help me do it!'" An honest seeker, she never said a word she didn't fully mean. She stirred her tea for a little longer after speaking of her prayer, and then continued. "I cannot explain it, but after I pray and when I start to sing, I know that quite literally I am not doing it by myself." I got to hear her in concert once. Her flowing presentation of sacred and secular songs awakened joy in over two hundred people.

From the Christian perspective, our human dependence finds its ultimate expression and greatest fulfillment in reliance on the living reality we call the Holy Spirit. The Holy Spirit is to be our teacher (John 14:26). We are to be born of the Spirit (John 3:5-8). We are to live by the Spirit and be guided by the Spirit (Gal. 5:25). In times of trial we are invited to lean on the Holy Spirit (Mark 13:11). These matters sounded strange to many who first heard them, and they surely can sound strange in our ears today. Nevertheless their realization remains as solid as the strength to follow through on a task we thought we could not handle, as staunch as the courage to take a difficult stand, and as nourishing as the wisdom to find our way through a harsh passage in life.

I find that I learn much whenever I watch those who live with dependence. Particularly in times of crisis they instruct and invite me. They put on no airs. They do not make me feel, as flashier public heroes sometimes do, that they are of a different order and all I shall ever be able to do is watch their unattainable feats. With their humble leaning, they point me to the Source of guidance and support that is available for me as well.

Openness

True humility opens outward. It expects and awaits. Those who seek to walk in integrity understand this truth. Knowing they shall never attain wholeness on their own, they grow hospitable. Acknowledging the incompleteness of their understanding, they welcome the ideas of others. This does not mean they adjust their thoughts to whatever prevailing winds of opinion may cross the widened threshold of their lives. They do not abandon their convictions. They evince, rather, the humility of the open-hearted and open-minded. They receive what comes their way, reflect, and seek to understand.

The humble, then, remain open to thoughts and perspectives different from their own. They do this not as a tactic to gain trust of others. Trust may indeed grow as a fruit of their openness, but they remain open primarily because they understand their own incompleteness. To put the matter theologically, they have learned that even on issues where they possess passionate feelings, they shall never fully know the mind of God. So they speak clearly and strongly whatever they have to say, but they also listen deeply. The act of listening will stretch their minds and at times will surely test their patience. It may lead to outright bewilderment: *How can these people feel this way?* Yet their listening continues, often with the inner prayer "What beckons here, Loving God? What are they, and you, seeking to say?"

> The humble remain open to thoughts and perspectives different from their own. . . . They have learned that even on issues where they possess passionate feelings, they shall never fully know the mind of God.

The genuinely humble remain open to correction. They do not withdraw from the person daring to say, "Good friend, you made a mistake." Nor do they turn aside from harsher criticism. And on this I must admit I find their example difficult to follow. If another gently suggests that I erred, I won't feel good about it. The more on target the reproach, the more likely I am to resist. Even so, the example of those more open to correction than

I continuously prods me. If the correction I have heard contains just a mite of truth, then I needed it. And if, as rarely happens, the correction holds not a speck of validity, at least I have been reminded that everything I do affects others, and they too have distresses and hurts.

The humble remain open to the gifts of others and do so with joy. They welcome with childlike wonder the singer's voice, the painter's delicate touch, the dancer's command of motion and space. They live out Paul's counsel, "in humility regard others as better than yourselves" (Phil. 2:3), viewing it not as a burden but as wise instruction. They look up to the insightful for their advice, the humorous for their gifts of laughter, the quiet for their gentle and nourishing presence.

Ultimately, on the broadest and most basic level, the humble open themselves to God's wider working. They live by an openness that says not "*I* have it" but "*You*, God, hold all, and though I cannot fully grasp everything that is happening, you are present in all that is here. You are tending. You are yearning. You can, if we will let you, shape us all."

■ ■ ■

FOR PERSONAL MEDITATION

♦ When I try to think of someone who lives with humility, who comes to mind? For what do I give thanks as I reflect on this person?

♦ Where have I been most prone to live the message "I have it"? Where have I grown most free to acknowledge my own limitations?

♦ Where have I repented, truly turning away from what does not work in life? Where do I need to engage in further turning?

◆ What have been special times of dependence for me? What have I learned in such times?

◆ In what way right now am I being called to greater openness toward other people and their gifts?

FOR GROUP REFLECTION

◆ Where do we see the "I have it" assertion played out in the world around us? . . . in the church? . . . in the places we move through in our daily lives? What do we believe gives rise to this assertion?

◆ This chapter observed: "To act with humility is in no way to cower or to hold back. Indeed, when it comes to acting on difficult issues, the humble often become the boldest." If each of us could tell about someone we have known who acted both boldly and with humility, whom would we discuss? What did these individuals do?

◆ What makes repentance difficult in today's culture? What makes dependence and openness difficult?

◆ Where in our society, and in ourselves, do we see the need for repentance? . . . for dependence? . . . for openness?

◆ When people look on the group(s) to which we belong, do they perceive a spirit of humility? What might we together do to further such a spirit?

◆ For what situations in the world do we wish to pray that there may be a greater spirit of humility? . . . For what situations in our nation? . . . in the church? . . . in our lives?

Chapter 5

Simplicity

IN JUNIOR HIGH OUR BOYS CHORUS LUSTILY BELTED OUT A ballad that included the words "What good is money? What can it buy?" The rest of the lyrics and even the title have long since passed from my mind, but I do know that in the final stanza we bid cheerful adieu to all worldly entanglements and committed ourselves to the delights of following the open road. Each time we sang the piece, we smiled broadly, pouring it out full throttle in spite of our cracking voices and an occasional wrong note. Indeed, what good was money? Never mind that by the world's standards we were at that moment warmly housed, comfortably dressed, and sumptuously fed. Never mind that if we actually did follow the open road, somebody somewhere would have to pay for the gas. We thrilled every time the choir director looked at us over the top of his glasses and, with a slight look of bemusement, instructed us to turn to that song.

As the years passed, of course, we began to get a different view of life. After not much more than a decade most of us were coming up with respectable answers to the question, "What good is money?" Well, for one thing, it was good for starting a family, if we were thinking about that. And it was good for education, if we were trying to pay it off. And of course there were cars and sporting events and movies and concerts and . . . the list went on. The high-spirited song faded into oblivion. It became as much a part of the past as the adolescent voices that sang it.

Yet as our culture labors its way into the new millennium, I detect something hauntingly pertinent in the idealism that pulsed through that young group so long ago. In light of the materialistic obsessions of our society today, do we even need to ask, "Have we gone too far?" I no longer stand among those junior high students. Much time has passed and I regard them from a distance. If at this moment, though, I were just once to hear them sing, "What good is money?" I would want to give them a cheer.

And I find myself asking a further question. When those twelve- and thirteen-year-olds sang with such abandon of a life that was blissfully free, did they in some way sense the self-inflicted pressures that would, in just a few decades, leave our culture panting to recover a deeper, richer spiritual breath? Even if their fervor sprang from nothing more than the perennial freshness of youth, it was, in retrospect, a poignant and prophetic fervor.

It has become a truism that we live in a time when persons increasingly yearn for a simpler way of life. This is not just a matter of wishing to live less bound to material possessions, though that is surely a part of it. The yearning surges forth in desires to have more time in life for the things that matter, even when fewer and fewer of us seem able to say what those things are. It throbs in heartfelt regrets that life has become too cluttered with obligations and too packed with competing desires to permit any room for joy.

In the church we are by no means immune to the longing for simpler ways. Indeed, we may long all the more keenly as we mourn the gap between the frantic pace of our days and the spiritual peace we proclaim. We know only too well that the institutional church frequently does more to augment hyperactivity than to assuage it. We have been naming the problem for years: "We are doing too much." "We need to focus." "Fewer meetings." "Simplify!" We remain, however, as addicted to complicating our lives as the society around us.

Against all of this clutter and drivenness stands a small, persistent body of persons. Some are lay; some are clergy. In the midst of life's harried complexities, they embody what the rest of us desire. At first glance, they rightly appear to be persons who have learned to say no. They set responsible limits and do not overextend themselves. As we examine them more closely, we realize that what they reveal runs far deeper than just the ability to establish personal boundaries. In the core of their being, they have heard the words "Every branch that bears fruit he prunes to make it bear more fruit" (John 15:2). Having heard this, they allow God's continuous pruning to take place. In the manner of those walking the way of integrity, they are of another country. They do not take their cues from our culture, which constantly urges all of us to possess more, do more, and be more. They draw both cues and life itself from the One who summons them to let go and live with greater simplicity so that they may embrace an even richer abundance.

For both the church and society as a whole, such persons emerge as true spiritual leaders. Amid today's crisis of mounting desires and plummeting satisfactions, they remind us of what we are to seek. Their ways among us tend to be winsome. They point us to many modes of simplicity, and I find that they challenge us to consider three in particular: simplicity of goods, simplicity of words, and simplicity of action.

Goods

Jesus speaks without equivocation of our relationship to the world's goods. We live in a time when it is both difficult and advisable to hear these words in full:

> Do not store up for yourselves treasures on earth, where moth and rust consume and where thieves break in and steal; but store up for yourselves treasures in heaven, where neither moth nor rust consumes and where thieves do not break in and steal. For where your treasure is, there your heart will be also.
>
> The eye is the lamp of the body. So, if your eye is healthy, your whole body will be full of light; but if your eye is unhealthy, your whole body will be full of darkness. If then the light in you is darkness, how great is the darkness!
>
> No one can serve two masters; for a slave will either hate the one and love the other, or be devoted to the one and despise the other. You cannot serve God and wealth.
>
> —Matthew 6:19-24

Jesus presses hard in two directions in this passage. First, following a negative but necessary trajectory, he announces that the quests for spiritual growth and for worldly treasure are perpetually at odds. One yields everlasting fullness and light; the other ends in emptiness. It simply is not possible to serve God and money. In the Gospel of Luke he puts the matter more flatly. A life devoted to accumulating goods is, ultimately, a foolish and shortsighted life (Luke 12:13-21).

Second, reaching far beyond the negative here, Jesus offers a vision of life in its fullness. This comes as a vision that our culture and the church ministering in it desperately need to reclaim. We are to set aside our pursuit of material things, Jesus says, and fill our lives with the treasures that quite literally will never fade, be taken away, or, in today's common scenario, become deadly boring.

As so often happens when we start to work with Jesus' teachings, the temptation with this passage is to catch the general drift of his words, then wander off into endless debates over what he really meant. Was he, perhaps, talking about our growing too attached to our possessions rather than about our having too much? And what about making wise preparations for the future? Jesus wouldn't be against that, would he? Our children often feel pressured to have the same possessions as their peers. How would Jesus deal with this situation? And how can we apply Jesus' teachings on the world's goods in the midst of an economy that does, after all, depend on a healthy amount of consumerism just to keep going?

The discussion of such questions can devour a lifetime. Some of the questions are thoughtful. Many represent little more than an effort to dodge the sharpness of Jesus' demands. With all respect to even the best discussions, though, I must say that I have found the clearest delineation of Jesus' teaching on the simplicity of goods not in words but in the lives of persons who have quietly gone about doing what he asked.

I think of a pastor I knew some years ago. She did not receive the highest salary in her ecclesiastical district. She had no hope of owning a little cottage getaway like some of her colleagues. The vacations she took with her family were modest. She planned carefully and, due to that, was able to provide adequately for her children's needs. Twice she turned down higher-paying positions, not because she had anything against a larger income but because she knew she was ministering exactly where she needed to be. Her life continued to grow rich in love, and though serving in the pastorate never became easy, her days pulsed with meaning. Simplicity had set her free.

I also think of a lay leader in a congregation I once served. His salary had never been particularly high, but due to his modest lifestyle he had the resources to give generously. His giving, like his life, was unpretentious. I knew about it only because from time to time he asked about various needs. He gave broadly: for the church, for mission work among the mentally distressed, for victims of this and that disaster. One night as we visited I tried to get him to talk about his reasons for giving. All he said was, "Oh, I like to do it," and then immediately told me about a fresh need he had learned of in a neighboring county. Simplicity had set him free for the treasures that would not fade.

In the end it is always the same. I encounter someone who lives simply with respect to the things of this world, and that person leaves me with a fresh set of questions. I no longer think about "What did Jesus really mean?" What he meant stands right there in front of me. So the questions turn personal. They press against the too-comfortable patterns of my daily life. Am I moving in the direction that this person and Jesus invite me? Am I letting go as I need to? Am I growing less encumbered by possessions, more generous, more open to the priceless gifts that surround us all?

Words

The challenge to attain simplicity of words is plain, easy to state, and daunting:

♦ Jesus never poured more words on a situation than the heat of the moment, or its dryness, called for. With him it was always "Let your word be 'Yes, Yes' or 'No, No'" and "Father, forgive" and "Render to Caesar the things that are Caesar's" and "When you are praying, do not heap up empty phrases." It was always "The kingdom of heaven is like yeast . . . good seed . . . treasure hidden in a field . . . one pearl of great value." Unadorned. To the point. He spoke and then just let the words go.[1]

♦ Here and there Jesus has some good followers of his approach. These persons have quit the need for verbal control, the rush of words, the desperate feeling that "Unless the idea comes from my lips and in my exact words, it hasn't been expressed." These persons listen a lot, speak little, say much. And after speaking they, like Jesus, let go of what they have said. They leave room for the Spirit to work, knowing that the Spirit will do things they never dreamed of.

♦ I don't think any more words are needed on this matter, but I do find myself wondering, *Can I ever learn to be as simple, as spare in my words, as Jesus?*

Actions

In contemporary filmmaking, attention once lavished on dramatic dialogue now surges, costly frame by costly frame, into the creation of dazzling action scenes complete with heart-stopping sounds for every fiery twist and turn. The higher the number of such scenes, of course, the greater the chance for a blockbuster at the box office. On television even the more contemplative sports, like baseball and golf, pack three plays into one, thanks to instant replay. And on the most personal levels, action-motivating questions can circle about us as tightly as hornets: Am I achieving all my objectives? If I've checked off one objective as done, with what new objective am I replacing it? Or better, with what two new objectives am I replacing it? I know I've got a lot going on right now, but wouldn't it look better on my résumé if I could list just two or three more activities? In such an environment, the measuring rod for the ideal life is a lengthy to-do list with many items crossed off, but never quite all of them. Actions themselves, vibrant and increasing in number, become the aim.

The lives of well-integrated, faithful persons present a different pattern. They aim not to do many things but to do a few things, or just one, well. For them "well" points not only to the quality of their work, which they desire to be the best they can offer. It points also to the intent. And they ever carry the intent that says, "O God, this is for you"; "Loving One, may what I do be one with your will"; "By your grace, may what I offer further your ways among us." They follow the pattern of Dorothy Day spending herself year after year to bring justice to the poor, and Desmond Tutu ceaselessly bridging barriers of hatred and discrimination. Theirs is the pattern of Paul passing three years in the wilderness and then, in ever-maturing ways, doing the one thing of telling others what he has found in Jesus the Christ.

The simplicity we see in the lives of those who walk in integrity has nothing to do with becoming passive or doing little. Such persons display a simplicity of focus. They honor the gifts and the gnawing call God has given them. And in light of both gifts and call, they shed from their lives everything that does not matter and give their all to what does. Their actions are spare, without waste, uncluttered, whole.

> Persons of integrity display a simplicity of focus. They shed from their lives everything that does not matter and give their all to what does.

For many of us the disparity between our daily lives and the call to simplicity of action is painful. I confess that when the pain arises for me, I often resist acknowledging the presence of any grace in my discomfort. In the end, though, I can neither dismiss the pain nor what it holds out to me. The pain reminds me that a life fractured by an overabundance of obligations is not the life for which any of us was created. It invites me to discern once again my few talents and how I may most effectively apply them. The pain grants me permission to say a clear "No" to anything that will dissipate my efforts. It offers license to yield myself joyfully to the few places that most need what I can bring.

And even as pain comes as a gift to awaken me, I find that the call to simplicity of action bestows a still greater gift: it encourages me. It does this every time I contemplate those who allow God's call to unclutter their lives. What they show me remains always the same. Healing love flows not in the helter-skelter or in the perpetual flurry but in the simple, focused act. It arcs outward in time given to a child or at the side of a bed, in the life lived for justice, in the sacrificial offering, in the act of unending prayer. The effect is more dazzling than any thunderous action scene wrought by special effects on the wide screen. It does infinitely more to heal the human heart.

■ ■ ■

For Personal Meditation

♦ Who has embodied for me the grace of living simply with respect to the world's goods? Who has modeled simplicity of speech? . . . simplicity of action?

♦ In what areas is my life too cluttered with things that really do not matter?

♦ Where in the past have I grown in the ways of simplicity? What aided me in the growth?

♦ Where do I most need to grow in the ways of simplicity?

♦ As a leader, am I living in a manner that fosters a larger awareness of simplicity? Am I encouraging greater simplicity in the organization(s) of which I am a part?

♦ For what shall I pray so that I may live more simply . . . so that I may encourage greater simplicity in the life I share with others?

FOR GROUP REFLECTION

♦ For each of us, who has modeled simplicity of goods? . . . of words? . . . of action? What fruit did simplicity bear in these persons' lives? What blessings did their simplicity offer to others?

♦ Where in the church do we see the need for greater simplicity?

♦ Of the three areas of simplicity treated in the preceding pages, which one do we believe cries out for the greatest attention in our society? . . . in the church? Or do all three areas need attention? What other areas would we name?

♦ What are we together doing to model the simplicity Jesus taught? What more might we do?

♦ In John 15:2 we read, "Every branch that bears fruit he prunes to make it bear more fruit." What would we pray that the Vinedresser prune from the community of faith? . . . from our own lives?

Chapter 6

Compassion

Room

IMAGINE FOR A MOMENT ONE SO SIMPLIFIED IN HER LIVING,
    so spacious in his heart,
  that this one now has room within
    for you in your hurt and
        in your weakness and
           in your fear and
  not only room for you, but growing room
    for others in their need and
        in their weakness and
           in their fear and
  not only room for them, but growing room
    for a world of need and
        weakness and
           fright.

And imagine for a moment the expression on her face,
    the caring look he leaves you
        as a memory

you know will stay
long after this person has gone
but really has not left you at all.

And imagine for a moment the wondering this one stirs
over the source and aim of
all the love that comes
and over whether your own heart might
one day become such
an ever-growing room.

For many of us the reflections invited by the preceding lines will draw swiftly to a focus. Somewhere we have met "one so simplified in her living, so spacious in his heart" that we felt as if we had entered an ever-growing room with space for our needs, for the needs of others, and even for the frights and terrors of the world. The memory of that person lives within us. It prods us to wonder at the love we experienced and to ask whether our hearts "might one day become such an ever-growing room." And even if we have never encountered such a person, our yearnings fill in the details invited by the poem.

To walk in the way of integrity is to grow in compassion. It is to live from the very One who is love. It is endlessly to make room. Writes the author of the First Letter of John, "Everyone who loves is born of God and knows God. Whoever does not love does not know God, for God is love" (4:7-8). Both the verb and the noun for *love* in this passage build on the Greek root *agape*, which speaks of divine love. This love reaches outward like the love that the waiting father shows the prodigal son as he limps home in his shame (Luke 15:20). *Agape* opens wide its arms; it joyfully welcomes. In the Hebrew scriptures, the psalmist sings of God's compassion: "As a father has compassion for his children, so the LORD has compassion for those who fear him" (Ps. 103:13). The Hebrew word for *compassion* derives from the stem *rechem*, which means "womb." Compassion mothers us. It protects, nourishes, and brings forth new life. The way of integrity invites us to offer forth this outreaching, receiving, life-giving love.

> To walk in the way of integrity is to grow in compassion, to live from the very One who is love. It is endlessly to make room.

Those who freely offer compassion do so sometimes against a background of wrenching need and sometimes in the very midst of it. They do so in crisis and in calm, in life's tempests and in seasons of quiet. They extend their care in the most intimate encounters and across the widest ranges of our human pain. In such persons the whole gracious enterprise springs from the ability to make room within themselves for others and from three interweaving elements of faithfulness that allow this loving room to grow: the self forgotten, the self found, and the ever-broadening family.

The Self Forgotten

Compassion grows in the soil of our self-forgetfulness. It expands in a space created when *me, mine,* and *I* step aside. In Matthew 15:32 we read: "Then Jesus called his disciples to him and said, 'I have compassion for the crowd, because they have been with me now for three days and have nothing to eat.'" In the Greek text the word for "have compassion" literally means "to be stirred in one's bowels." In Jesus' day people spoke of the bowels as the center of kindness, affection, and yearning for others in much the same way that today we speak of the heart. To have compassion was to let this absolutely central place of life become filled no longer with the self and one's own needs but with the needs, hurts, and longings of others.

Our English word *compassion* bears no direct linguistic link to words of the biblical text, but it gives voice to the same human experience. *Compassion* derives from the Latin words *com* and *pati*. It literally means "to suffer together with." To have compassion is to open oneself fully to the pain of others, even to the point of having that pain at the center of one's being.

To have compassion in the full biblical sense is also to act. It is to reach out. Those who dwell at the center of a person's life now become the object of that person's deeds. Thus, moved by compassion, Jesus feeds the famished crowd (Matt. 15:32-38), cures the sick (Matt. 14:14), touches the eyes of the blind (Matt. 20:34), and teaches multitudes that have been living as sheep without a shepherd (Mark 6:34). For the compassionate, action no longer focuses on the self but on others in the midst of their pain.

In our day, when someone acts with compassion the effect can be stunning. I do not mean this cynically and am not claiming that acts of compassion are now so rare that they shock us when we see them. I suspect there has always been and always will be something stunning about compassion. We live in a time, though, when self-fulfillment touts itself as a god, and self-absorption increasingly comes forth as the singular fruit of striving after this god. In this setting, even the quietest lives of compassion offer a grace-filled and daring contrast.

I once watched a man take an unusual step. Given another chance, he would, I am sure, take it again. A leader in his congregation, he also was the president of a medium-sized company. During a lean year he cut his salary to ensure that not even one employee lost a job. Amid the ebb and flow of the national economy, he reduced his salary several times. As he neared retirement age, he took a further step. He received a buyout offer from a larger firm. The terms, though highly lucrative for him, left workers unprotected. Without hesitation he declined the offer. Two years later he sold the firm, for substantially less personal gain, to a group willing to guarantee the positions of all his employees. He simply refused to hold these persons and their families anywhere other than at the center of his being.

To forget self may mean forgetting one's finances and status. It also mean forgetting time. The compassionate know how to ignore the clock. They set aside the hurried "I have to run along now." They know how to stop and open their hearts and ears. They receive with love the story that needs to be shared and take upon themselves the pain that another can no longer bear alone. At times they sit for a long while in silence, affirming the infinite worth of the person who sits, or lies, nearby. However it happens, *me, mine,* and *I* cease to dominate life's core. In the space created, something fresh begins to form.

> The compassionate know how to ignore the clock. . . . They know how to stop and open their hearts and ears.

The Self Found

Consider for a moment two expressions of a further element in the life of compassion. The first of these comes to us from another era. The second is contemporary. Neither by itself gives a complete picture. Taken together, they suggest a reality we need to claim.

In 1919 Calvin Laufer penned the words to the second stanza for his hymn of Christian service "We Thank Thee, Lord":

> We've sought and found Thee in the secret place
> And marveled at the radiance of Thy face;
> But often in some far-off Galilee
> Beheld Thee fairer yet while serving Thee.[1]

Nobody sings this fine hymn much anymore. *Thee* and *thy* echo a mode of speech seldom heard today. Mention of some far-off Galilee no longer summons the host of positive images so readily available in Laufer's more romantic age. Still the basic declaration of the lines rings clear: "Christ, wherever I serve, you are right there. I see you full and fair!"

The second expression took place not long ago. Six of us—family and close friends—had seated ourselves around the bed in a hospital room, simply waiting, as one does in such situations. The aged figure in our midst lay in a coma. A physician had rightly told us, "It's only a matter of time." An order of nuns had founded the hospital, and at one point an elderly member of the order appeared in the doorway to the room. She was dressed in a fashion none of us had seen in years. Her full-length habit covered all but the tips of her black shoes. Her oval face looked out from the tight frame of her wimple. Tall and lean, she held herself absolutely erect. I must confess that, for reasons neither laudable nor fair, I hoped her visit would be brief.

The nun walked over to the bed. Slowly she leaned forward and took hold of the old man's hands. She spoke just a few words first to him, then to his closest kin. I cannot remember what she said, but as she spoke, two extraordinary things happened. First, those of us seated around the room received an immense and completely unexpected sense of being lifted. It was as though we were all being upheld by and through her. I am convinced that, in some way beyond our understanding, the good person who lay in our midst knew the same lifting. And second, there was what happened to the woman's face. To say that it softened would be accurate but falls short of expressing what we saw. To say that she offered an infectious, wholly unself-conscious smile would also be right, but this description too is less than adequate. The closest words to describe what happened would be to say that her face now radiated life. That life stayed with us and warmed us when, after not more than three minutes, she passed out the door and on down the hallway.

For me this woman's face shall forever embody the truth that sings through the words of Laufer's hymn. For a brief time that afternoon, we were her Galilee. Forgetful of self, she entered the room. There, at the center of her being, she made room for us and for all the pain, waiting, and wondering she saw. She made space for *agape*, the divine and outreaching love. And the life that radiated from her face? What was it but the life of one who in the very moment of self-forgetfulness was finding once more her true identity? What was it but the glow of one knowing again that "Christ, you are here. In the love that surrounds us, fills us, and calls us forth, you are here. This is the life we are made for"?

Compassion not only empties us but leads us to discover that we are vehicles for the love that knows no limit. It begins to fill us in ways that extend beyond anything we might imagine on our own. "I came that they may have life, and have it abundantly," said Jesus of all who would follow him (John 10:10). The abundance Jesus offers has nothing to do with the accumulation of the world's goods. It is not about position or prestige. His abundance, on the other hand, has everything to do with the cries of hurt and pain that surround us. It has everything to do with discovering once again how we have been fashioned to open ourselves to one another's need.

The Ever-Broadening Family

The prophets of Israel possessed what many of their time found to be an irritating habit. In the name of the Lord God, they persistently widened the boundaries of what people ought to be concerned about. None of them did this with greater force than Isaiah. Speaking to a people who at least on the surface professed a desire to live more faithfully, he offered an unequivocal word from the Lord:

> Is not this the fast that I choose:
>> to loose the bonds of injustice,
>> to undo the thongs of the yoke,
> to let the oppressed go free,
>> and to break every yoke?
> Is it not to share your bread with the hungry,
>> and bring the homeless poor into your house;
> when you see the naked, to cover them,
>> and not to hide yourself from your own kin?
>
> —ISAIAH 58:6-7

These well-honed phrases sliced as neatly as a knife through any easy pieties. Do you really want to do what God chooses? Then shatter the injustice around you, free the oppressed, feed the hungry, and draw the homeless into your own dwelling. Jesus' life and teachings advanced this theme without letup. In birth he came to the poor and needy. At table he welcomed those whom pious folk shunned. Women, children, tax collectors, Samaritans, and Roman officers counted for nothing in the world that surrounded him, but Jesus made room for them all. And in nearly his last act of teaching, Jesus packed a parable with a festering mass of hungry, thirsty, needy, and naked folk. Then he made it clear: The life eternally blessed is precisely the life that stretches outward to welcome persons such as these (Matt. 25:31-46).

This constant widening of love's boundaries shapes the life of compassion. The person who walks in closeness with God may be a longtime walker or just taking the first tentative steps. This person may be a prophet, an aging nun, a searching teen, a stretched pastor, or a lay leader trying to live the faith in some wretchedly difficult setting. Whoever the person is, it all comes down to the same elemental movement of the spiritual life. This person seeks to live in closeness with the One who is perfect love. And the divine love she meets, the limitless compassion he encounters, invariably stands ready to expand the bounds of even the most saintly life. Compassion will always have more sisters and brothers to introduce to us, more parents, more children, more flesh of our human flesh for us to receive, to stand with, and to cherish.

For most of us the broadening of family under the tutelage of divine compassion elicits the same range of responses that can greet any family addition. At times we thrill. At times we struggle and groan, "You mean I really have to love those over there as well?" Of course we know the answer even before we ask the question. And we know too what we have learned from watching persons whose love outreaches our own. Their lives are indeed spacious and abundant. In the midst of many hurts, they offer healing. Where the crises of social and economic turmoil reign, they lead toward liberation and justice. Losers of self and finders of self, they create an ever-greater room. We look on them and always they draw us back to the same question: Will we allow such room to grow within us?

■　■　■

FOR PERSONAL MEDITATION

♦ What persons dwell in the room of my heart right now? What is special about each of them? What do they give me by their presence?

♦ Where have I suddenly seen the face of Christ while opening to the needs of others?

♦ Where am I now being asked to let the room of my heart grow wider, more inclusive of others and their needs?

♦ What of *me, mine,* and *I* do I need to let go of in order to love more fully?

♦ Who has made room for me and my needs? What qualities do I give thanks for in these persons? What truths do they have to teach me now? What encouragement do they offer?

For Group Reflection

♦ If we could each choose just one person who, for us, exemplifies compassion, who would this be? What did this person do?

♦ Where have we seen persons dare to live out the guidance offered in Isaiah 58:6-7?

♦ Where have we seen others awaken to the abundance of living that comes from opening to one another's need? Where have we awakened to that abundance ourselves?

♦ When persons look at the church, where do they see compassion? When persons look at our group, where do they see compassion?

♦ How, both in the community of faith and in the wider culture, can we encourage greater openness to one another's need?

♦ What habits of self-centeredness do we need to break in society? . . . in the religious community? . . . in ourselves?

♦ What prayers would we request—and what prayers would we offer—so that our own lives, and the life we share in community with one another, may become an ever-growing room?

Chapter 7

The Capacity for Lamentation

THREE CRIES FROM LONG AGO LINGER IN MY MIND. THEY sounded in my childhood and have echoed through the upper reaches of middle age. I expect they shall never completely leave me. Were they to do so and free me of their discomfort, I am sure I would lose more than I would gain.

The first cry came from behind me as I lay on a couch watching television. The only other person in the room was my grandmother. I was in third grade, and we were inspecting the newfangled, picture-producing box that had replaced a couple of old chairs in my parents' living room. An early version of the evening news played out before us when suddenly we found ourselves in the midst of violence half a world away. People threw things, hit one another, and fired shots not fifteen feet in front of us. Some fell to the ground. That is all I recall of the visual. What most took me came from the voice at my back. "Oh . . . oh . . . *oh!*" My grandmother sounded as if she had been hit. She grew silent as the unexpected mayhem gave way to a commercial.

Then she spoke once more, very slowly. "Will we ever, ever learn?" I didn't try to answer. I cannot recall anything from the remainder of the evening.

The second cry arose in our church nearly a year later. Our pastor read scripture superbly. By that I mean that whenever he read, he got out of the way of the text. So what I really heard one day shortly before Easter was a bewildered Jesus calling out, "My God, my God, why have you forsaken me?" I remember badgering my parents about this later. Did Jesus really say something like *that*? The words, weighty and fierce, pressed in my mind.

The third cry came after the passage of another year, and I saw rather than heard it. I was at summer camp. Early one afternoon the sky blackened, lightning snapped, and winds buffeted the immense pines of the northern Wisconsin forest. And, unbelievably, ancient trees fell. All of this happened in a matter of minutes. After the storm passed, counselors hurried the campers in our division up to the recreation hall, where they kept us busy most of the afternoon. Late in the day we went back to our cabins, but only for a short rest, and then were ushered up to the dining hall. Following dinner the camp director told us that one small camper, just two cabins down from my own, had died in the storm. We left the dining hall in silence. The cry that I recall was as mute as it was perfectly shared. A cabinmate of the child who had died left the hall weeping. Around him were the arms of his nineteen-year-old counselor. He said nothing but simply held the boy close and shared his tears.

After all the years that have passed, the recollection of these cries still brings me distress. Too much sudden pain remains in the first of them, too much anguished wondering in the second, and too much sheer sorrow in the third for their long-lingering echoes to do anything else. And somehow even as a child I suspected that these persons were, at the moment of their cries, dwelling in a realm that I myself might one day need to enter.

Those who walk in the way of integrity neither shun nor deny the existence of life's fiercest pains. In the most searing crises, they possess the wisdom to enter the pain and lament what they find. At times pouring out their sorrow appears to be all they do. Yet, even though they themselves may not realize it, they lead in a direction the rest of us would do well to follow. With the fullness of their lives they show the absolute need for lamentation. They honor the absolute freedom God grants us to express our anguish. Quietly, they demonstrate that true lamentation leads to a greater, healing closeness in the divine-human bond.

> The true spiritual leader knows the absolute need for lamentation. In the harshest circumstances that person leads because she dares express the sadness.

Absolute Need

The true spiritual leader knows the absolute need for lamentation. In the harshest circumstances that person leads because she dares express the sadness. This one, and this one alone, opens fresh ways because he is not afraid to speak of the darkness.

For several generations now a sound secular wisdom has advised us against repressing our feelings. We are all familiar with the lines of thought sustaining this counsel. Society and early training may say to us, "Don't cry." The customs of family or clan may admonish, "Don't embarrass us with your feelings," or "Keep it to yourself." We human beings, though, shall forever strain against such limitations. Our eyes do not lose the ability to shed tears when we turn eight years old. The sixty-year-old voice is just as capable of shrilling out the cry of grief as is the voice of an infant. At times it desperately needs to. Even as we catch a firm whisper from within telling us, "Hold back your feelings," we also hear, "You shouldn't keep them in. Your pain will only grow worse." We sense the prudence of this latter counsel.

The absolute need for lamentation encompasses this secular wisdom but also reaches beyond it. To lament is to *ex-press*, that is, to *press out* of oneself the sorrow for the wounds one sees. These may be wounds to one's own self, to the vast body of humanity, or to one's very sense of the presence of God. Those who risk open lamentation not only give necessary vent to pent-up feelings. They move toward the only realms where healing can begin, and they do so on several levels.

First, on the most commonly acknowledged level, the person who dares to lament can most completely reach out to others in their pain. This does not mean that the pain of the person reaching forth must be identical to the pain of the one hurting. And it certainly does not mean that whoever bandies the popular phrase "I feel your pain" has connected with anything beyond his own vocal cords in pronouncing those words. However, those dwelling in a place of anguish instinctively sense the genuineness of another who has also dwelt in that place. Sensing this genuineness, they know they are no longer alone. This is why, in times of personal lament, the most important responses often come not through any outpouring of words but through an understanding gaze, the touch of a hand, or a silent embrace. And this is why, in times of deep public loss, a leader's race to hurry everything back to normal can leave completely untended the spiritual wants of an entire people. In both private and public sorrow only those who acknowledge the fullness of loss can meet others and abide with them in their need.

On a further level, often the person with the courage to lament awakens others to deep pains in the wider human family. This role may be far from popular, but it is utterly essential. The awakening must take place if the world's wider wounds are ever to enter the glow of a more healing light. To lament publicly the clouds of economic injustice darkening the world's poor is in no way to lift those clouds. Issuing sharp cries over genocide in the shadows of war or openly mourning mass extinctions in the depths of a vanishing forest neither ends the horror nor stems the loss. It does, though, make a desperately needed beginning. Those who lament beam the light of awareness exactly where it needs to shine. They do so even if at first the light startles and offends others. Were they to suppress their lamentation, no awareness would exist at all, and not even a hope of healing.

On a further level still, those who dare lament draw us into a place of healing where we may be most reluctant to go. As we grieve the condition of someone we love, or strife in an organization we cherish, or an unfairness that has shattered our trust, we find questions now press hard from within: *Where indeed is this One who reaches toward us? Does this One reach at all? God, are you even here?* Rather than stifle their wondering, those who lament fully voice their sorrow. In their bewilderment they honor the one reality of the spiritual life that still seems to greet them: their absolute freedom to pour forth all they carry within.

> Those who lament beam the light of awareness exactly where it needs to shine.

Absolute Freedom

In the scriptures faithful folk find no limits set on what they can say to God. They understand that the living God has granted them freedom to express their distress, and they exercise this freedom to the fullest. If we listen thoughtfully to the biblical words, we begin to hear this all-encompassing freedom:

> As a deer longs for flowing streams,
>   so my soul longs for you, O God.
> My soul thirsts for God,
>   for the living God.

When shall I come and behold
    the face of God?
My tears have been my food
    day and night,
while people say to me continually,
    "Where is your God?"

—PSALM 42:1-3

This freedom allows the faithful to express deep longing, as in the words just shared. It permits them to cry out against isolation and even to accuse God:

O LORD, God of my salvation,
    when, at night, I cry out in your presence,
let my prayer come before you;
    incline your ear to my cry.

For my soul is full of troubles,
    and my life draws near to Sheol.
I am counted among those who go down to the Pit;
    I am like those who have no help,
like those forsaken among the dead,
    like the slain that lie in the grave,
like those whom you remember no more,
    for they are cut off from your hand.
You have put me in the depths of the Pit,
    in the regions dark and deep.

—PSALM 88:1-6

Exercising this freedom, a psalmist may pour forth impatience:

How long, O LORD? Will you forget me forever?
    How long will you hide your face from me?
How long must I bear pain in my soul,
    and have sorrow in my heart all day long?

How long shall my enemy be exalted over me?
Consider and answer me, O LORD my God!
                                        —PSALM 13:1-3

Drawing on this freedom, a faithful soul can even wonder at
abandonment:

My God, my God, why have you forsaken me?
    Why are you so far from helping me,
        from the words of my groaning?
O my God, I cry by day, but you do not answer;
    and by night, but find no rest.
                                        —PSALM 22:1-2

Such words do not sound softly in the ear. For some persons,
except for the fact that these words appear in sacred texts, they
press well beyond the limits of accepted piety: *Well, yes, I appreciate the opening of Psalm 13, but I'm not sure I could ever say
such a thing myself.* As a pastor I more than once heard anguished, faithful folk replicate the cries of abandonment
sounded in the psalms of lamentation, only then to see well-
meaning friends try to talk them out of saying "faithless things."

Yet such shattering of limits by faithful persons can instruct
us and, ultimately, encourage us. Biblical scholars note that the
psalms of lament comprise nearly one-third of the book of
Psalms. That is not an idle piece of information. It is a keen observation on the nature of the faithful life. Those who seek to
walk in wholeness with God know times of deep distress, and in
these times they fully express their sorrow and anguish.

The Divine-Human Bond

Ultimately, lamentation leads to a greater, healing closeness in
the divine-human bond. The cause of sorrow may not recede.

The trial that evoked the cry may not end. The cry itself may yield no pathway of escape from harsh reality, nor should it be expected to. Lamentations come always from the lips of those who face the harshness, not from those trying to turn away. Still, as the cry pours forth, it opens wide the spirit of the one who issues it. And in this opening the greater closeness grows.

The psalms of lament provide a clear portrait of one change that occurs. Even where the outward crisis remains unresolved, an inner assurance begins to return. The faithful person who cried, "Will you forget me forever?" closes with:

> But I trusted in your steadfast love;
>> my heart shall rejoice in your salvation.
> I will sing to the LORD,
>> because he has dealt bountifully with me.
>
> —PSALM 13:5-6

The one for whom "tears have been my food day and night" concludes with a three-time repeated refrain of rising trust:

> Why are you cast down, O my soul,
>> and why are you disquieted within me?
> Hope in God; for I shall again praise him,
>> my help and my God.
>
> —PSALMS 42:5, 11; 43:5

And the one who called out, "My God, my God, why have you forsaken me?" at length proclaims the restoring goodness of God:

> For he did not despise or abhor
>> the affliction of the afflicted;
> he did not hide his face from me,
>> but heard when I cried to him.
>
> —PSALM 22:24

In such psalms, as in our own lives, change does not always come swiftly. The souls who wrote these texts struggled no less than we do. It appears, however, that at some point their very being breathed with the sense that *Yes, God, you are here. Even now, even in the midst of this, you are here.* This realization, for them, proved sufficient for moving forward.

Greater closeness in the divine-human bond comes in another, more demanding form as well. The psalms of lamentation are a great gift, but they are not the only lamentations in the scriptures. Prophets repeatedly bewail a nation that no longer lives in the ways of God. Jesus sorrows over a religious leadership that delights in the honors it receives but neglects justice, mercy, and faith (Matt. 23:1-24). He weeps for a Jerusalem that has not a clue of what will bring it peace (Luke 19:41-44). These lamentations turn ever outward. They focus on injustice and dislocation in the human family. The space they create for the deepening of our bond with God summons us to walk into the world-wounds spread before us.

The spiritual leadership of those who openly lament is indeed a strange thing. I suspect that at the moment of their lamentation, leadership lies far from the thoughts of such persons. Nevertheless, it happens. The "Oh . . . oh . . . *oh!*" of an aging voice implants a sound that will not vanish. The arms of a nineteen-year-old man around a weeping child leave an abiding image. The cry of a dying Savior stirs an uneasiness that, through all the ages, has never fully passed away. We wonder at such matters. And in time we realize that the sound, the image, the profound uneasiness come from those who, with absolute authenticity, call us to venture further on faith's demanding and, at times, painful way.

▪ ▪ ▪

FOR PERSONAL MEDITATION

◆ Who has shown me the freedom God gives us for lamentation? What have I learned from watching this person?

◆ In what situations have I known the absolute need to lament? Where have I exercised this freedom? What growth or change came as I exercised this freedom?

◆ In what places now, in my own life or in the world around me, do I sense the call to lament?

◆ Where do I need to grow freer in expressing to God my sorrows and deep distress? What might I pray for so that I can grow in this freedom?

◆ In situations where I am called upon to lead, how can I more fully model the freedom to lament?

FOR GROUP REFLECTION

◆ Where in our society, and in our personal lives, have we seen the absolute need for lamentation? Where have we seen the absolute freedom exercised?

◆ Where in public and political life do we feel the need to lament has been honored? Where do we believe the need has been denied or cut short?

◆ Where do we right now sense a need for lamentation in society as a whole? . . . in the church?

◆ What can we do to encourage greater openness to lamentation in the wider church and in any particular church bodies to which we belong?

◆ Over what situations right now do we wish to offer prayers of lamentation?

Chapter 8

The Capacity for Joy

O God,
you are the well-spring of life.
Pour into our hearts the living water of your grace,
that we may be refreshed to live this day in joy,
confident of your presence
and empowered by your peace,
in Jesus Christ our Lord.
Amen.[1]

—*BOOK OF COMMON WORSHIP: DAILY PRAYER*
The Presbyterian Church (USA)

THIS PRAYER COMES FROM THE LITURGY FOR MORNING prayer in my own community of faith, a small part indeed of the whole body of Christ. I have no idea how many follow the liturgy strictly. Given the tendency of Presbyterians to be conscientious to a fault, I like to fantasize that it is more than just a few. And so on Thursday mornings, the fifth day of the week and therefore the most probable day for using prayer 5, which this prayer is, I occasionally envision a vast mob of us praying that, by God's grace, we will live the day in joy. Some of us pray in formal services, some over the breakfast table, some in the privacy of a study. I enjoy thinking that a few exceptional souls may even offer the prayer in a taxicab, on a commuter train, or while inching along the security line at an airport. Maelstroms may await us, or a day of glossy smoothness from start to finish, or impossible colleagues, unexpected horrors, equally unanticipated honors, or five meetings, all of which we absolutely must attend. Into the known and the unknown we plunge. We do not have a lot of control over what's out there. "May we, O *please*, *God*, be refreshed to live this day in joy."

I have always liked this prayer, particularly the phrases "pour into our hearts the living water of your grace" and "confident of your presence and empowered by your peace." The words remind me that, as I pray for joy, I reach toward a reality independent of the movements of any given day. Joy, if I experience it, will put me in touch with something deeper than just the normal ups and downs of circumstance, even if for the moment I cannot say precisely what this something deeper is.

Certain folk, by the way they live, teach us what joy is all about. These joy bearers are not jokesters. Almost never would they be called the life of the party. Still less frequently do they chirp, "Cheer up" in the midst of disaster. Yet they possess the quality rightly called joy. They live that joy as much in the midst of crisis as they do in days of outward celebration. Walking the way of integrity, they carry within them one of the great paradoxes of faith: The person of faith both laments and rejoices mightily. In perfect parallel to the part of their nature that knows the need for lamentation, they embody the absolute need for joy. They honor the absolute freedom God grants us to pour forth our joy. And they clearly reveal that living into joy strengthens the divine-human bond.

Absolute Need

We live in a culture that values happiness, often in its most exterior and fleeting forms, but knows little of joy. This simple fact of our existence delineates how deeply we need joy.

The word *happiness* derives from the Old English root *hap*, meaning "chance" or "fortune." In its early uses, to be happy was to have good "hap" or luck. Happiness, whenever it arose, resulted from some favorable external circumstance. It came from situations people could point to and say, "There. Look at that. I'm happy." This quest for items both favorable and external motivates much of life today. We can seek the perfect body, or the powerful position, or the spirit-lifting possession, whether for the moment this possession happens to be a new car, a new computer, or a new partner. To attain such we are endlessly encouraged to improve ourselves, to plot a smooth trajectory from one exciting goal to the next, and of course, to buy. If disaster strikes, we are urged, by an article of faith propounded from even the highest levels of public life, to shop our way back to normalcy.

> We live in a culture that values happiness but knows little of joy.

We know all too well the outcome of such dependence on outward "hap." Perhaps the addictive quality of pursuing "hap" allows our society to decry the shallowness of this perpetual chase, then do little to disengage from it. Even so, the truth of the matter persists. The latest purchase grows outmoded before the season's end. The goal just achieved pales before fantasies of higher attainments. The interpersonal relationship believed to be trouble-free turns out to be like any other relationship: it requires work. The religious fellowship newly joined and thought to be squabble-resistant and a bit of heaven on earth still manages to squabble. In no place is it possible to say for long, "There. Look at that. I'm happy." Disillusionment sets in, emptiness returns, and the hungry quest begins again.

The word *joy* opens whole new realms for consideration. Whereas happiness relies on the outward and the immediate, joy prods us to look deep within. The word *joy* comes to us from the Latin *gaudia*. *Gaudia* did not depend on chance events and external acquisitions. It pointed to an internal, abiding sense of well-being. Outward and immediate blessings might well quicken the heart. They could appropriately stoke particular fires of one's joy. But to speak of joy itself was to tell of a reality more intimate, and far more sustaining, than any emotion dependent on outward events. To speak of joy was to give voice to a steady exaltation of spirit at the very core of one's being.

In both the Hebrew and the Christian scriptures, joy describes more than just a deep inner state. It is a state that consistently finds its source in the living God. Those who know joy heed the words spoken through Isaiah: "Be glad and rejoice forever in what I am creating" (Isa. 65:18). They sing with Paul, "Rejoice in the Lord always; again I will say, Rejoice" (Phil. 4:4). In the voice of the ancient chronicler they trace all blessings back to their beginning: "All things come from you, and of your own have we given you" (1 Chron. 29:14). Those who know joy in the full biblical sense live in steady communion with the Creator of all their days.

Or there is another way to put all of this. Happiness sits by the window, in front of the computer, or by the phone. It waits for some good event to call it into being. Joy has no need for such waiting. Because it draws life from the Giver of all life, joy does not depend on outward circumstances. If some particular goodness comes, joy may celebrate wildly, but it never relies on external goodness. And whenever self-centered waiting and narrow pursuits pinch life into emptiness, we see how absolute is the need for joy. "Hap," in short, will never fill our lives. "Gaudia" will both fill and lift them.

Absolute Freedom

One bright spring afternoon during my third year in seminary, I nearly crashed into an older gentleman standing stock-still in the middle of the stairs located on the hill behind the chapel. As I rapidly descended he had his back to me and his head cocked to one side. From the dignified silhouette I recognized him as a missionary who was home on brief furlough from Sri Lanka.

When I shot past he blurted out, "I just heard an indigo bunting!" Unable to check my momentum, I turned and caught a glimpse of his face. His eyes glowed, and his left ear appeared glued to a tree outside the women's dormitory. I uttered something no more profound than "Wow!" and continued my charge down the hill. That was the last time I ever saw the man. For more than thirty years now I have been trying to hear an indigo bunting on my own.

> Those who know joy in the full biblical sense live in steady communion with the Creator of their days.

The freedom of the joy bearers in this world is the freedom of an unself-conscious child, a delighter, and a reveler. This freedom shatters all the boundaries of normal expectation. And so King David dances mightily before the Lord as the ark returns to Jerusalem (2 Sam. 6:12-23). *How shocking! I can't believe he's doing that!* Jesus delights in the company of the unsavory (Luke 5:29-32; 7:36-50; 15:1-2). *How shocking! Does that man have any idea what he is up to?* A courtly man casts shyness to the winds and to a hurried stranger declares the loveliness he has just stopped to hear. *Did he really say what I thought he did?*

The joy bearers live free from excessive piety. About the time I discovered the attractions of the indigo bunting, a friend pointed me toward some unexpected words from the writings of Dietrich Bonhoeffer. I liked them instantly and have come to appreciate them more and more with the passage of the years:

> Speaking frankly, to long for the transcendent when you are in your wife's arms is, to put it mildly, a lack of taste, and it is certainly not what God expects of us. We ought to find

God and love him in the blessings he sends us. If he pleases
to grant us some overwhelming earthly bliss, we ought not
to try and be more religious than God himself.[2]

The truly joyful do not stifle celebrations with a hasty, "Let's be
quiet now and pray." Their full entrance into joy is itself a form
of prayer.

The joy bearers freely declare the eternal source of their joy.
They do this boldly in deed and word. They also do it through
the quiet, unmistakable movements of countenance and heart.
King David danced openly to the Lord. Jesus delighted in the
ragtag folk gathered around him and in Abba, who embraced
them all. The smile on the older man's face not only proclaimed
his joy in the song of the bunting but told of the infinite goodness he heard moving through that song. The joy bearers forever
instruct us, reminding us that we have the absolute freedom to
proclaim, "This goodness, it is of God!"

If we closely watch the true joy bearers, they show us still
more. Their freedom to express joy extends to realms where a
shallower vision of life would tell us no joy exists. Enter deeply
into joy; seek it through the dark nights and across the deserts
of the soul, the joy bearers tell us. Eventually we come to the
place where we will pray with the faithful of the ages: "Yes, God,
you are here. In my weakness, you have sustained me. In my
grief, you have been at my side. Even when I wondered and
wandered, you would not let me go." To pray like this is to move
into the very heart of where the joy bearers would lead.

The Divine-Human Bond

The joy bearers ultimately draw us into a place of great growth.
With their struggles and their simple affirmations they remind
us that dwelling in joy has nothing to do with skipping lightly

from one source of giddiness to another, nor even with resting on solid attainments such as competence in one's field, honors, or material security. As we watch the joy bearers, we see that they live ever more fully from an inner awareness that the Loving One is with them in all realms, even the most frightening and fierce.

An aging and imprisoned Paul wrote:

> I have learned to be satisfied with what I have. I know what it is to be in need and what it is to have more than enough. I have learned this secret, so that anywhere, at any time, I am content, whether I am full or hungry, whether I have too much or too little. I have the strength to face all conditions by the power that Christ gives me.
>
> —PHILIPPIANS 4:11B-13, GNT

Paul's carefully chosen words suggest he did not reach contentment all at once. He had learned through the years. Through struggles, shipwrecks, and threats. Through betrayals, beatings, and long nights of wondering what would become of the latest church to slide into turmoil. Bit by bit, knowledge and understanding came to Paul. Joy grew. He realized, *Loving One, you are here.*

A friend voiced this realization not many years ago. After nearly a decade of pastor-parishioner battles and ever stronger reconciliations between us—after times of reaching out to each other, trying to understand, then stumbling and trying to understand again—we were visiting for what we knew would be our last time. The next day I was leaving for a new ministerial call a thousand miles to the west. She lay flat on her back in the hospital, the heart monitor above her head flashing an unsteady signal. At the moment of "Good-bye" she took my hand. "I'll see you again," she said.

We paused, conscious of the monitor, aware of distance and of time. At length she spoke once more. "And if I don't see you again, well, I'll still see you again!"

As I walked out of the hospital a few minutes later, I knew her words had arisen from something infinitely more genuine than a need to fill the silence between us. She was too honest for anything like that. Behind her last words to me, and permeating the smile that accompanied them, lay eighty-five years of learning. She had learned in the midst of extended crises, some of which included the loss of her husband, son, and farm. She had learned in seasons of open celebration. Whatever the day might bring, the Source of true joy would continue to sustain her. She was confident now. And who could say how everything would turn out? Not I. Not she. But however gently or starkly the next crisis might come, the Source of true joy would be present too. The living water of grace would flow. In the mystery of God's workings, in ways beyond the power of either of us to comprehend or express, she—and would I dare claim this for myself?—would surely see.

▪ ▪ ▪

FOR PERSONAL MEDITATION

◆ Who has most fully shown me what it means to live with joy? What has this person taught me about living though times of crisis?

◆ What distractions turn me away from seeking the fullness of joy?

◆ Where have I grown most open to joy? Where have I grown most free in expressing joy?

◆ In times of crisis what most helps me ground myself again in the living God—what prayer? . . . or verse of scripture? . . . or activity? . . . or music? . . . or poem? . . . or image?

◆ Through the years, where have I grown in the sense of inner assurance? Where am I perhaps being called to grow in that sense now?

♦ In situations where I am called upon to lead, how am I helping to create time and space for us to explore our joy together?

FOR GROUP REFLECTION

♦ This chapter observed: "We live in a culture that values happiness, often in its most exterior and fleeting forms, but knows little of joy." Where do we see signs of the truth of this statement? Where in particular do we see signs of the need for deep joy?

♦ If we could each name one person who has lived with a sense of joy, who would that person be? In what particular ways did this person exercise the absolute freedom to express joy?

♦ In the family of faith, how can we encourage one another to share our joy more fully?

♦ How can the church help the wider society awaken again to the fullness of joy, even in the midst of crisis?

Chapter 9

Endurance

THOSE WHO WALK IN INTEGRITY ENDURE MUCH. THEIR quest for wholeness will not permit them to do anything else. When I think of endurance, I shall forever remember a ninety-two-year-old man making his way up an indoor stairway to worship in the church he had attended for decades. He labored just ahead of me, climbing two steps and then pausing for a long time, then three more steps and pausing again, then two more steps. With his left hand he held onto a railing; with his right he clasped the arm of a younger friend moving beside him. I caught the old man's face in profile whenever he turned and nodded "stop" or "go ahead." At the bottom of the stairs someone had asked, "Wouldn't you like to take the elevator?" to which he quipped, "No. The last time I took it the dang thing got stuck." Then he focused on the stairs.

When he reached the top, the old gentleman straightened, turned toward his friend, let out a huge sigh, and gave an absolutely beatific smile. Then he focused on moving forward again. Taking what must have been a thousand tiny steps, he progressed about two-thirds of the way toward the front of the sanctuary, nodding to the many who greeted him. He eased down into his pew, smiling once more. Never mind that in an hour he would have to go through the painful process all over again.

I had come to the church as a visitor that day. I knew the man somewhat by way of reputation, and his reputation played through my mind during the service. As the civil rights struggle mounted in the 1960s, he, an inner-city teacher, became an outspoken supporter of racial equality. He never abandoned this cause, even as years passed and others seemed to forget. For as far back as anyone could remember, he had urged his church toward greater involvement with the poor and the homeless of its immediate neighborhood. Both inside and outside the congregation he advocated for improved care for the mentally ill. In his early eighties he took on environmental concerns. None of this had been easy. His commitments demanded much time. Over the years he encountered periodic upwellings of misunderstanding and hostility. Still, he kept on.

After the minister pronounced the benediction, the friend who had accompanied the old gentleman up the stairway asked if he might prefer to take the elevator on the way down. Okay, he'd try it. I am not sure how the ride went, but the next time I saw him, he was back on the stairs. Two steps at a time, then three, then two, pressing and pulling all the way to the top.

If the sacraments are, as many say, an outward and visible sign of an inward and invisible grace, then this man's movements flowed with their own form of sacramental grace for anyone fortunate enough to see him. Struggle . . . smile . . . pain . . . pause . . . focus . . . more pain . . . smile . . . and through it all, keeping on, keeping on. A wonderful wholeness passed in front of us here. The man's body had become an outward expression of the spirit he had nurtured within since before most of us drew our first breath. And what he had tended within through so many wider efforts now provided its own support for the struggles of body and flesh. Even though I understand that this gentleman eventually became bedfast and lost all ability to communicate, I am sure that in some manner beyond our human capacity to calculate such things, his steadiness continued until for him all was complete.

> In the biblical vision, those who seek wholeness do not flee the pain that comes upon them. They endure.

"The one who endures to the end will be saved," Jesus says in Matthew 10:22. This bold statement runs counter to prevailing sensitivities in many circles. Endurance seems little valued today, especially the endurance of anything unpleasant or degrading. The word *saved* also can pose a problem. *Saved? What is Jesus getting at here?* we may wonder. Yet what Jesus is getting at and the endurance itself are vital in Jesus' teachings. They appear inextricably bound. On whatever level we choose to wrestle with the matter, the salvation Jesus speaks of is nothing less than the word implies. It is the *salvus*, the ultimate and eternal health. It is being made forever whole. It is both the end point and the birth into new life for those who live with integrity. And those who find it must endure.

Endurance and Pain

The pain endured by those who walk with integrity most often takes shape as a pain of the spirit. It may begin as an inner ache that arises from being severely misunderstood or misrepresented. The pain can mount under the pressures of ridicule and outright rejection. Because even legal and physical threats may be involved, it may sometimes assume the shape of genuine fear. Even if the bearer of such pain possesses a high threshold for discomfort, that person will nonetheless grieve over all the energy lost to conflict and distress.

Those who endure such pain do so across the full range of human experience. Some protect the environment. Others struggle for economic justice. Still others seek, with fairness and much personal agony, to lead organizations through times of traumatic change. Some speak for the full rights of persons who are denied them due to the color of their skin, their gender, or their sexual orientation. Still others, in the midst of escalating conflicts, urge the stillness and empathy needed if harmony is ever to return. However well such persons carry themselves, at some point they know the sting of hostile words. Or, even worse, they see the cause to which they have devoted themselves largely ignored.

Physical pain may accompany the pains of spirit. Persons who undergo pains of the spirit may encounter corporal abuse. In the most horrendous circumstances, they may have to bear some violation of the body along with everything else they carry. To say this is not to be overly dramatic. It is simply to acknowledge a sad and continuing fact of our human condition. Further, physical problems may arise as a result of the emotional pummeling. Bodily exhaustion and illness come all too often as war wounds in the struggle for justice.

The biblical response to pain knows nothing of denial and avoidance. In the scriptural understanding, the pains of both body and spirit are absolutely real. They appear to come with particular force on those who seek to walk in integrity before the living God. Queen Vashti gets banished for refusing to put her beauty on cheap display (Esther 1:10-20). We do not hear of her again. Jeremiah gets lowered into a cistern where he sinks in the muck. It is a half-ridiculous, thoroughly humiliating image (Jer. 38:6). Jesus, for all his efforts to heal both body and spirit, must finally struggle in the garden of Gethsemane and die on the cross.

In the biblical vision, those who seek wholeness in the human family do not flee the pain that comes upon them. They endure. At first glance their example appears far less reassuring, and certainly less appealing, than all the easy words that promise nothing but prosperity for those who walk in the ways of God. What these faithful sufferers show us, though, bears the mark of honesty. Because they do not shun even the harshest realities, they exude an authenticity that practitioners of avoidance and denial can never claim. Sometimes they must do this through the very long haul.

Endurance and Time

More than a little truth comes through in the waggish comment "The only real problem with endurance is that it takes so much time." We like our crises to end quickly. We prefer uncertainties to clear up in just a day or two. We wish our discomforts to leave us, if possible, in a matter of hours. All this is understandable. We naturally want the distressing aspects of life to hurry past and be gone.

A serious problem arises, however, when the movement toward wholeness requires long expanses of time, and rather than take the time, we wish to shortcut the process. We then fall prey to what Rabbi Edwin Friedman labeled "the quick-fix mentality."[1] The quick-fix mentality pretends a solution is reached when none has been achieved. It claims, "That is behind us," when nothing has changed. Confronted with genuine ambiguity, the quick-fix mentality opts for dogmatic certainties and simplistic answers. It blames another person or nation, demonizes another religion or race, rather than seeking to understand. The quick-fix mentality slams shut the windows of the mind when widespread hurts cry out for openness and commitment to long-term, prayerful search. Wherever the quick-fix mentality reigns, taking time becomes a problem. Whenever we submit to this mentality, we literally cannot abide time.

The link between endurance and time poses an additional, even more serious problem. An injustice that lasts one hour has already consumed sixty minutes more than it should. If that injustice persists for generations, or even just a month, people have every right to cry out in utter bewilderment, "How long will this go on?" It may well be true that "suffering produces endurance, and endurance produces character" (Rom. 5:3-4). But how much character is needed before children cease being denied basic rights due to the color of their skin? How long shall thousands starve each day while the resources of their land are siphoned off to feed the wealth of an already satiated caste half a world away? For how many years must innocents die as "collateral damage," bombed at weddings or work or as they come out of the temple, the mosque, the synagogue, the church? Even a second of such time endured is too long.

On the matter of endurance and time, the Bible offers no simple answers or swift solutions. It presents real people who, whatever may happen, keep striving for what they know will be better. In the roughest and most unjust circumstances, those who seek wholeness continue. Jeremiah grows utterly weary, decides to quit, but finds he cannot stop saying what

> Those who endure draw their capacity to endure from two primary sources: the community of faith and the living God in whom they ground their life.

he knows he must (Jer. 20:7-9). Jesus' effort to draw humankind back into the richness of God's ways extends to his last prayer of mercy from the cross (Luke 23:34).

In softer, less pain-wracked events, the Bible's link between endurance and time remains the same. Abraham and Sarah hear God's promise of abundant blessing, but from the start they know that fulfillment lies far in the future. They must journey and endure (Gen. 12:1-3). In the Gospel of Luke, Anna and Simeon wait and watch for the promises of God to be accomplished. They yearn for fresh life to come to a faith weakened by division and loss of zeal. When something finally happens, they have persisted in their devout yearning for decades (2:25-38). The Bible's answer to the problem of endurance and time is not to explain it away or make light of it. The response is to point to those who keep on . . . and keep on . . . and keep on.

Those who live with integrity embody the biblical approach to endurance and time. They know in their hearts that every major historical movement toward justice began with the courageous efforts of a few and came to fruition after much time. They understand that achieving resolution on a difficult issue or finding fresh vision for what lies ahead will almost invariably take time. They are the Wesleys bringing the gospel to the poor. They are Saint Francis, Luther, Calvin, Ignatius, and Teresa of Calcutta, all of them acting in the crises of their days and bringing light into realms of darkness. They include the pastor I knew who came to a divided church for three years, stayed ten, and left a legacy of unity and mission that has lasted for twenty. Among them is a quiet laywoman who spent fifteen years building an organization that shelters scores of persons each night and feeds hundreds in a city not far from where I live. For all these persons nothing happened quickly. And the question that their manner of living poses for us is, How, then, shall a person endure?

Endurance, the Community of Faith, and God

I have watched those who endure. Some of them surrounded me as a child. A number are my colleagues in ministry, and still more are members of congregations I served as pastor. In my better moments I have tried to learn from them. What they have shown me is simple, though in no way simplistic. They draw their capacity to endure from two primary sources: the community of faith and the living God in whom they ground their life.

On the journey of faithfulness we are not meant to walk alone but in community. From the book of Genesis onward, God makes covenant not just with individuals but with a people. In continuing this covenant, Jesus invites his disciples not only into

a relationship with him but also into fellowship with one another. Indeed, he reminds them that their mutual love will signal
to others that they are his disciples (John 13:35). The movement
toward wholeness in this world calls forth the deeds of individuals, but ultimately this movement is to be shared. We are to depend on and support one another.

Any who have sought support from the community of faith
know that this support is imperfect. The support, like the community itself, can falter and disappoint. When lived to its fullness,
however, this same support overwhelms us with goodness and
lifts us anew. The support may come as a call in the evening: "I'm
thinking of you." It may appear in an unexpected note we receive
or take shape in the touch of a hand. It can arise as we remember
another who once endured what we are enduring, and the memory reminds us, "You are not alone." Or the support may come in
the knowledge that even now many others are enduring as we
are. However it arises, the support of the community of faith
abides with us. We lean on the community. The community stays
close as we endure both the time and the pain. It helps us continue even when we do not fully see what lies ahead.

A further and fuller support attends us. The prophet Isaiah understood firsthand the demands on any who sought to ground their
lives in the living God rather than in the gods of society or self. He
declared to all faithful strugglers the ultimate source of aid:

> Have you not known? Have you not heard?
> The LORD is the everlasting God,
>   the Creator of the ends of the earth.
> He does not faint or grow weary;
>   his understanding is unsearchable.
> He gives power to the faint,
>   and strengthens the powerless.
> Even youths will faint and be weary,
>   and the young will fall exhausted;

but those who wait for the LORD shall renew their strength,
    they shall mount up with wings like eagles,
they shall run and not be weary,
    they shall walk and not faint.

—ISAIAH 40:28-31

Even the strongest among us shall weaken. Not only can the all-out race exhaust us but also the long, steady walk, the difficult movement day after day. Our aid, says Isaiah, is the One who fashioned us and the entire creation. To this One we can cry in our weariness, "O God, help!" Before this One we may wait in silence, utterly still and open and needy. Then, in both miracle and mystery, this One shall renew us so that again we may soar and run and walk . . . until . . . without shame . . . we lean on the One and the community again.

I sense that the old gentleman who leaned on a friend and struggled up the stairs in front of me understood all of this with every fiber of his being.

■ ■ ■

FOR PERSONAL MEDITATION

♦ Of whom does the man at the start of this chapter remind me? What do I give thanks for in this person? What do I most need to learn from this person?

♦ Where in the past have I needed to endure? What aided me? What might I learn from this experience that can help me now and in the future?

♦ Where in my life right now am I being called to endure? And what might I pray for so that I can endure?

♦ Where, as a member of the community of faith, have I been

able to help others endure? And where might I offer that help now?

For Group Reflection

♦ What pain have we seen others endure as a result of living with integrity? What sustained them? Where have we seen others endure through time, and what sustained them?

♦ Where have we endured pain as a result of living with integrity? Where have we endured through time? What sustained us?

♦ Where has the community of faith failed to help persons endure? Why? Where have we seen the community help persons endure? How did it do this?

♦ In what arenas of life do we hear the call to endurance today? What can we ourselves do, and model for others, in response to this call?

♦ For what particular gifts do we pray so that we can faithfully endure?

Chapter 10

Honesty

"WHERE ON EARTH HAS ALL THE HONESTY GONE?"

The question popped out of a girl two rows over from where I sat waiting to catch a plane. Since such expressions generally belong to people over fifty, her youthful tones startled me. I looked up and lifted my eyebrows. There she stood, half smiling, half frowning. She had just verbally stamped her foot. She had done this rather loudly too, as I saw several other gray and balding heads look in her direction. Possessing a proper sense of the dramatic, she next did what most good foot-stampers do: She turned and walked away. I had no chance to ask, "But what do you mean?"

"She's eleven," her mother called out for any to hear.

"And thinking!" I responded, then dug back into the day's paper.

After a minute I quit the paper and started to muse. What had set her off? Today's all-too-steady flow of scandals in business, academia, politics, and the church can set the mind spinning. Had the airport TV just blatted something about another

CEO making millions while employees lost their jobs and honest shareholders their hopes? Had that pushed her over the edge? Had something happened at school, or had she spotted fresh misdeeds in the newspaper that she had carried off tucked under her arm? I wanted to find her and say, "Look, it's not all that bad. Just view yourself in the mirror. Think of your best friends and your neighbors down the street. A lot of you are trying. You really are." Then I thought, *No, let her keep her anger. Something good may come of it.*

I caught sight of her walking back toward her mother. She held a partly consumed candy bar. Before I could smile and call out, "Thanks," a gravelly voice announced boarding privileges for rows nineteen and up. She disappeared into a sea of taller, wider forms.

As our plane lifted off, I found the young girl's outburst drew my mind toward an additional question. I have asked it myself, though I confess I have done so less often than I ought to. Its precise expression takes differing forms, but the question always boils down to this: How can I maintain my honesty in the place I find myself right now?

At some point this question emerges for nearly all of us. We ask it when others' behavior compromises our cherished values. We ask it as we wonder, *How much should I say? When should I say it? Should I say anything at all?* We also ask the question when our deepest beliefs make us uncomfortable with patterns of group behavior we have too long accepted. *Do we need to change here? Do I need to change? How can I stay true to what I see must be done?* Or as we battle circumstances that have surged beyond our control, the question may take shape in agonized wondering: *How can I keep my honesty and sanity* and *my job?* As we articulate such wondering we may realize that, for the sake of both honesty and sanity, we need to let go of the job.

Behind these questions lies the perception that, on some deep and abiding level, honesty still counts. The young girl acted on this perception when she asked six rows of innocently waiting passengers to grapple with what had suddenly gripped her mind. You and I honor this perception whenever we struggle with how to stay honest when we find ourselves in a tough spot. In such circumstances, honesty has hold of us and we have hold of it. We do not want the bond to break.

The way of integrity affirms the importance of our struggles here. Integrity in its fullest sense points us toward wholeness with God and with one another. In light of this truth, the age-old approbation of honesty remains essential for our health as human beings. When honesty fails, we rightly cry, "Where on earth has it gone?" When we strive for honesty even though the effort may cost us dearly, we act on our best instincts, not naïveté. Without honesty, the bonds between us shatter and integrity dies. If we forfeit honesty, we sacrifice any chance at wholeness of spirit. If, however, we seek to maintain honesty, if we mourn its absence and strain for its renewal among us, then we seek soundness of life for our society, its institutions, and our own day-to-day lives.

> If we wish for an increase in the world's honesty, we must start with ourselves.

With this "Amen!" of encouragement, the way of integrity offers further perspectives.

Honesty with Ourselves

Integrity sets forth a primal lesson: If we wish for an increase in the world's honesty, we must start with ourselves. To use a phrase once offered by Quaker leader Douglas Steere, we need to "begin from within."[1] We may become distressed over betrayals of public trust. We may agonize over the wounds that the duplicity of another has inflicted on us or on someone we love. Nothing in the way of integrity teaches that we should ignore the wrongs incurred through dishonesty. At the same time, for those walking the way of integrity, any quest for honesty will start with a focus on matters far closer than even the most searing external wrongs.

Jesus' counsel from the Sermon on the Mount offers particular help here:

> Why do you see the speck in your neighbor's eye, but do not notice the log in your own eye? Or how can you say to your neighbor, "Let me take the speck out of your eye," while the log is in your own eye? You hypocrite, first take the log out of your own eye, and then you will see clearly to take the speck out of your neighbor's eye.
>
> —MATTHEW 7:3-5

When I first reflected on these words, I heard Jesus barking them out like an overstressed supervisor. As I grow older, he speaks them more gently. Either way, his message remains the same: Start with the self. "And as far as honesty goes," he seems to tell me, "only if you are honest with yourself will you have an authentic word to speak on the need for honesty in the lives of others."

I know all too well my capacities for self-deception, and I find that Jesus points me toward a much-needed arena of self-examination. What is the congruity, or lack of it, between my boldest affirmations and my deeds? Am I living what I say about the treatment of others? about the treatment of my family? of the poor? of my coworkers? Do I embody what I so easily profess about openness to persons different from myself? about generosity? about care for the creation? about being straightforward with others as I pass through a day? I can easily slide into patterns that do not match my rhetoric. Am I living in the manner I claim to?

I believe that, in this driven age, Jesus directs us toward another area of self-examination: Are we being fully honest about our deepest spiritual needs? For many of us even naming our spiritual needs does not come easily. We have received little training in the matter. Our culture constantly encourages us to declare the needs we can touch, buy, and possess, but it provides no instruction in articulating the needs of the soul. Deep within us, though, the needs continue. They will not simply fade away. To grow in wholeness, we must attend to them.

So we must ask ourselves about the needs of the spirit that cry from within. Does rest beckon? or solitude? or play? Or does our greatest need of spirit surge forth in the desire to nurture some special talent we have too long neglected? And what about the overall shape of spiritual growth in our lives? What fresh form does growth now seek to take? Does the need to grow draw us toward some slight outward change in life? Or does it demand a major change? Such questions stretch us. Responding to them will stretch us even more.

At the very least, beginning the quest for honesty within reminds us how difficult the whole quest can be. And how long-lasting. I have not discovered a final answer for any of the above questions. For that matter, I haven't met anybody who could check off all such questions as over and done with.

The more we attend to our own honesty, the more clearly we perceive that honesty shall always beckon to us from fresh realms. We shall never fully possess it. The best we can hope for is to keep growing. This humbling insight does not come as the only lesson integrity holds for us in the midst of today's crises of public and private honesty. It does, though, mark a vital starting point.

Honesty with Others

Although integrity counsels that we begin our quest for honesty from within, it also directs us to be completely honest about what we see around us. It does so across the full range of human experience. The scriptures know nothing of the thought that says, *If we will all just focus on ourselves, everything will be fine.* In an ideal world, that might work, but humanity has not managed to fashion such a realm. So Amos denounces the wealthy in Israel for selling the needy for a pair of sandals (Amos 2:6), and Jeremiah decries religious leaders who popularly proclaim, "'Peace, peace,' when there is no peace" (Jer. 6:14; 8:11). Those who seek wholeness speak openly about what they see.

Jesus does exactly that. He chides Sadducees for failing to understand the power of God (Mark 12:18-27), rebukes Pharisees for neglecting justice and the love of God (Luke 11:42), and upbraids his disciples for their slowness of belief after the resurrection (Luke 24:25-26). Jesus does not just bore in on the negative. He speaks the forgotten, stunning truths about who we are and how God works among us: "You are the salt of the earth. . . . You are the light of the world" (Matt. 5:13, 14). "In fact, the kingdom of God is among you" (Luke 17:21). He points to children and says that the kingdom of heaven belongs to such as these (Matt. 19:14). After the wealthy pour loud, clattering offerings into the temple treasury, he gestures toward the widow who just slipped in two thin coins and says she gave the most because "she out of her poverty has put in all she had to live on" (Luke 21:1-4). Jesus steadily lives this lesson: In the midst of life's confusions, false pieties, and just plain forgetfulness, only honesty can clear a path wide enough for wholeness to return.

By no means are those who dare obey honesty's prodding confined to the pages of scripture. In my first parish a young parent sought me out one afternoon and, in spite of his obvious discomfort, told me face-to-face of a serious hurt I had caused. For the sake of a shattered bond, he ventured forth.

Years ago I knew a fine woman who served on several community boards. On two of these boards she encountered major cases of financial misconduct. Shy, she dreaded confrontations. She agonized over what to do, but both times she raised the issue without fanfare and with great effect. Despite the personal pain involved, she reached out with her honesty.

And I recall once stifling a grin, though I should have stifled nothing, as I heard a middle-aged man speak honestly to a large group. On a sweltering June night over one hundred members of a notoriously reserved congregation filed into a fellowship hall to hear a speaker. As a visitor, I listened with them. The speaker's words connected with us on a level no one quite expected. The listening grew deep. At the end everyone looked around at a few key figures who nodded, indicating that, in this instance, modest applause would be appropriate. Once the applause subsided, and that did not take very long, the man stood. "Excuse me," he said, looking over the whole dripping bunch of us, "but before we go I need to say . . . well, I think we've . . . well, we've, uh . . ." Then he blurted it out: "We've actually had an experience of the Holy Spirit here." Utter silence greeted this comment. Then came nods of *Yes, yes. So that's what this has been!*

To be honest means to speak forthrightly about what we see across the whole range of our experience. It means talking openly about the hurts we see—the slights, the dishonesties, and the searing injustices. It means being just as direct about the surprises, the goodness, the ways we witness God working. It means telling of the sudden and holy delights. If we practice such honesty, we take a step that will lead in directions as disparate as correcting a friend, declaring our distress with widespread unethical practices, or proclaiming, "God is in this place."

I personally find the step of being completely honest with others to be among the most demanding footfalls on the way of integrity. If I see that I need to take this step, I often grow anxious. *How shall I say anything at all? How shall I begin? How can I form my words in such a way that they will be heard? And if others reject what I say or reject me, how will I handle it?* I suspect I am not alone in such wondering. And here again, those who have walked the way of integrity have much to teach us.

Honesty Offered with Love

A simple trait stands out among those who speak honestly and do it well: They speak with love. They follow Paul's counsel to offer even harsh truths with love so that all may grow together into a single, united body (Eph. 4:15-16). They know that the arrogantly offered correction may satisfy the speaker but rarely changes anything. When persons of integrity speak, they desire not to dominate or humiliate but to aid and bring forth wholeness for everyone. Whether they must share honest words with just one other or with many at once, they act from an inner prayer that has already asked, "Loving One, may what I now share serve to build up all of us."

For many such persons I suspect their loving tone arises in part from having looked honestly at themselves. Knowing their own weaknesses, they extend to others the same compassion they wish to receive. The young parent who years ago told me that I had hurt another put this clearly when we talked several weeks later: "I hated like anything to correct you because I know how often I need correction myself." The habit of beginning from within had set him free. Free from arrogance. Free from superior tones. And free therefore to communicate, without any hindrance at all, his genuine concern for my behavior. I could have rejected what he said, but the barrier between us would have been entirely of my own construction. His loving humility bridged my defenses and ultimately broke them down.

Of course matters do not always come out as we desire. Barriers do not always fall. We choose our words with care, but others refuse to believe. Or they just shrug their shoulders and keep on as usual. We see our best counsel cast off and perhaps find ourselves discarded as well. When this happens, speaking the truth in love appears, at least for the moment, to have been far more costly than effective.

Here, precisely at the point where honesty costs the most,

Paul's admonition to act with love can aid us once more. When Paul urges us to speak the truth in the spirit of love, he again uses *agape*, the word for divine love, the love that comes from Abba, the giver of all wholeness, to whom even Jesus turned repeatedly in prayer. Paul asks that as we speak honestly we root ourselves in this love. And when we depend on the Loving One, we move to the very center of integrity's path. We enter the place where young girls cry, "Where on earth has all the honesty gone?" and maturing folk agonize over, "How can I maintain my honesty now?" We reclaim our chosen ground. Whatever may happen, we know that we shall be upheld and shaped by the only One who can ultimately make us whole. Such knowledge will not take away the pain of rejection. It will, however, grant us the perspective of knowing that, even amid the pain, we are exactly where we need to be.

■ ■ ■

FOR PERSONAL MEDITATION

♦ Who have I valued for displaying honesty in difficult circumstances? What did honesty cost that person? What did he or she gain? What did others gain?

♦ When have I willingly paid a price for being honest? What did honesty cost me? What sustained me as I paid the cost?

♦ Where have I seen others speak freely about goodness and holy delights and what they see God doing? Where might I do so more freely myself?

♦ Where in my life right now am I called to greater honesty?

♦ Who has, in love, spoken a difficult truth to me? How did this person approach me? In what ways do I wish to grow more like this person?

◆ As a leader, how am I helping honesty grow within the groups of which I am a part? What more might I do?

FOR GROUP REFLECTION

◆ Where in society at large have we seen honesty set aside? Where in the family of faith have we seen it set aside? And where have we seen it affirmed and practiced, even at great cost?

◆ What fears or enticements make honesty difficult to maintain right now? In the face of these, what is our prayer?

◆ In the family of faith how can we encourage the pattern of speaking the truth in love? How can we more fully support those who suffer for their honesty?

◆ Where, both personally and as a community of faith, do we most need to speak honestly today? For what shall we pray as we seek to do this?

Chapter 11

Prophetic Living

THOSE WHO WALK IN INTEGRITY ENGAGE IN PROPHETIC LIVING. They declare, by both word and deed, God's yearning for justice in all of humankind and God's healing intent for even the most intimate realms of daily life. They live in the manner of the prophets of Israel, who dared offer a fresh vision of what life was to be about. The prophets did this in the midst of national crises, struggles for religious identity, and long seasons of cultural and moral decline. Early Christians dared to do the same. So it has been through the ages. In times of confusion and pain, persons who walk with integrity steadily challenge those around them to see what life can truly become.

Those who live prophetically do so day to day, issue to issue. Though their vision extends beyond the boundaries of time, they focus much of their energy on the close at hand, the now, the immediate. We brush up against them in the supermarket. We sit across from them at board meetings, next to them at worship. Their manner of living does not belong just to the well-positioned and the famous. Prophetic living comes forth as the call of common, down-to-earth folk. And as Jesus showed when he praised a Samaritan for his barrier-shattering kindness, often down-to-earth folk—even persons that the religious community shuns—take the lead in prophetic living (Luke 10:25-27). When I reflect on those who live prophetically, I think of an elderly woman in a small New England town, a high school math teacher I knew long ago, and a pastor.

I can still see the elderly New England woman arch her eyebrows. Arch her eyebrows, and then follow up with a polite but firm, "I don't agree with what you just said" and a full explanation of why she did not agree. This never came as a completely automatic reaction on her part. She always paused and thought a bit first. But if somebody made an anti-Semitic remark or cast aspersions on others because of race, gender, or what side of the tracks they lived on, you could count on it. She would stare straight ahead for a moment, then up went the eyebrows and out came the comment. She nettled her friends by doing this but also expanded the minds of the young.

The teacher adored mathematics and gave his best efforts to sharing this passion, even among those of us for whom he couldn't possibly have held out much hope. He clearly had other passions too. I remember him singing lustily in church, though his vocal abilities were about on a level with those of us who weren't doing well in his math classes. Once I saw him march in silence for racial equality; years later I heard that, as a proud and devoted veteran, he demonstrated for peace. Twice in our algebra class, in rare diversions from his lesson plans, he asked us to "ponder the fact that everybody deserves a good math education. What, then, might we do about

Those who live prophetically do so day to day, issue to issue. Though their vision extends beyond the boundaries of time, they focus much of their energy on the close at hand.

the terrible disparity between our affluent suburban district and the strapped inner-city districts?" Somewhere deep within himself he harbored a wider than normal vision of the economy of God's love. Not every adult in our community liked this man. "He's complex," I heard one of them mutter with a shake of the head. Many of his students, though, sensed something good in this complexity.

Over the years the minister served as pastor in two markedly different situations, one in the inner city, the other amid extreme rural poverty. In each setting this person radically broadened the understanding of others, doing so with genuine humility. Through time both churches developed strong ministries to shunned and hurting persons in their neighborhood. Members began to grasp the connection between problems seething on their doorstep and wounds, open and untended, around the globe. Of course some parishioners did not want to hear about the wider hurts or that they themselves bore any responsibility for what happened half a world away. "That's not what we come to church for." On a somewhat different line, the pastor urged congregational and denominational leaders alike to look at new forms the community of faith could take. Some paid scant attention. At least a few began to listen.

> Those who live prophetically create discomfort. . . . They willingly risk the rejection of others when only such risk can open the way for change.

With gratitude I must say that I have encountered this pastor a number of times. He used to be older than I. Now I find her looking remarkably young, although sometimes she comes along with graying hair and moves at a pace no faster than my own. I never know quite where I will next run into this person. I do know that were I to inquire, "Have you accomplished all that you wished?" I would hear in response a quiet, "No. I'm afraid not." If I were to go a little further and ask, "Has your work ever gotten you into trouble?" I would hear, perhaps with a laugh, "Oh, heavens, yes." Then again, at times I would hear no laugh at all. I also know that if I were to turn away from the pastor and ask others, "Has this person marked your life with a fuller sense of God's justice and love?" more than a few would respond, "Yes. Indelibly."

Those who live prophetically create discomfort. This, in part, explains why they prove so effective in the long sweep of history. They willingly risk the rejection of others when only such risk can open the way for change. They become the first few to venture into some new territory of need. Wherever they find themselves, they press for wider awareness. They stand forth as harbingers of much-needed transformation. And if we look on them closely, we come to see that they act not as the partisans of some passing political ideal or momentary social program but as the bearers of an infinitely rich and living reality.

Bearing the Goodness That Is to Come

"Here we have no lasting city," writes the author of Hebrews, "but we are looking for the city that is to come" (13:14). The writer of this intense and stunning letter of encouragement makes it plain that the city to come is nothing other than the city whose architect and builder is God (11:10). It is the heavenly city where all life shall be complete and whole (12:22-24). Those looking for this city do not just sit and wait. Like Christ, they go outside the comfortable confines of life as they now know it (13:12-13). They confess Christ's name, do good, and share what they have (13:15-16). In short, those looking for the city even now bear its goodness into the world.

The letter to the Hebrews sounds one of scripture's earliest and most persistent themes: Amid the world's brokenness and chaos, God promises goodness; those persons who root their lives in God bear that goodness with them. For Abraham and Sarah this means carrying the promise of God's blessings as they set out for an utterly unknown destination (Gen. 12:1-3). For the prophets and those listening to them, hearing God's promise and bearing its goodness persistently intertwine. The prophet Isaiah declares:

> They shall beat their swords into plowshares,
>   and their spears into pruning hooks;
> nation shall not lift up sword against nation,
>   neither shall they learn war any more.
>
> —ISAIAH 2:4

Micah speaks the same promise and then extends the vision:

> Nation shall not lift up sword against nation,
>   neither shall they learn war any more;
> but they shall all sit under their own vines
>   and under their own fig trees,
> and no one shall make them afraid;
> for the mouth of the LORD of hosts has spoken.
>
> —MICAH 4:3-4

For those who truly hear Isaiah and Micah, their words not only offer hope but become a source of guidance. Those who take the prophets' words to heart carry the promised goodness back into the world. They act daily for the coming of God's shalom.

The Gospels portray the same pattern. On being told of the child she will bear, Mary sings her gratitude to God:

> He has shown strength with his arm;
>   he has scattered the proud in the thoughts of their hearts.
> He has brought down the powerful from their thrones,
>   and lifted up the lowly;

he has filled the hungry with good things,
    and sent the rich away empty.

                                        —LUKE 1:51-53

Mary sees something utterly new breaking forth. As the child she gave birth to begins his ministry, he proclaims that the reign of God is at hand (Matt. 4:17; Mark 1:15) and then spends three years attending to the poor, the weak, the forgotten, and the shunned. Jesus bears into this world the goodness that is coming. At the end of his ministry, he teaches that anyone who follows him must do the same (Matt. 25:31-46).

In our own era, as in any other, those bearing the goodness that is to come look squarely at the needs around them. They hear the cries of the forgotten, the poor, and the abused. They lament divisions among nations, among faiths, and within the church, but they do not stop at this point. They also lament the lack of humility that feeds and sustains our human brokenness. They dare to look within themselves, their society, and their nation to see the factors contributing to this brokenness. As they scan the world about them, they sorrow too for the loss of forests, coral reefs, and stillness in the human heart. They grieve the widening gap between the few who have more than enough of creation's abundance and the many who must scratch and pick their dusty way from one season of life to the next. They rejoice in compassion wherever they find it. However, they never sentimentalize the goodness they see. Nor do they allow life's dazzlingly bright moments to blind them to the harsh realities they must keep in view.

As they look on the needs around them, those who live prophetically ask questions. Not spectator questions. Not speculative questions, such as, "What do we think is going to happen next out there?" or "Who will respond this time and what might they do?" Instead, they ask questions of deep personal involvement, such as, "What is God trying to teach me here?" "What fresh hurt pulls at me?" "To what injustice must I now give my time, energy, and substance?" "Where am I being asked to further the wholeness God yearns to bring among us all?"

Obviously those who live for the goodness that is to come face demands. They must endure much. Yet if we watch them closely, neither the demands nor the endurance impress us so much as one further and lasting element.

Confidence

Sometimes the old and the wise most fully reveal what lies at the heart of prophetic living. Sometimes the very young, humbling us, do the same. I once startled a fourteen-year-old boy when I caught him praying in the sanctuary of a small church where I served as a summer intern. He had disappeared from a youth group meeting in the church basement. He was not gone for long, perhaps ten minutes, but I had ventured into my first solo effort as a pastor, and I got nervous quickly.

The church sat on a hill far out in the country. I went outside and called the boy's name. No answer. This left the sanctuary as the only other possibility, and though I did not expect to find him there, I thought I'd better try. His head popped up from a bowed position in one of the pews as I walked noisily up the aisle. He smiled.

"My gosh, I'm sorry to bother you," I said.

"No, no. That's all right," he responded. He smiled again, then stood up and hurried back to the youth group. I would like to say I know exactly what he was praying about, but I didn't ask. I'd like to indicate I learned what passage of scripture he had focused on in the Bible that I saw him slip back into the pew rack, but I did not find that out either.

I did know that six weeks before, just ahead of my arrival for the summer, his mother had died without any warning of ill health. One day she bounded through all her usual chores. The next morning she collapsed and never made it to the hospital. I knew too that this young person, like almost all others his age, wrestled with a host of personal choices and outside pressures, none of which was easy to resolve.

As the summer passed, I came to see that this quiet fellow possessed an uncommon grace. He continued to deal with his own crisis of grief. In the life he shared with his peers, several times he made courageous behavioral choices. Through all of this he offered a gentle confidence. He offered it more by how he carried himself than through words, though occasionally he spoke of it. Quite simply, he evinced a trust that all the good things he cherished and held to would in some manner continue. More than continue, they could never be blocked or taken away, not even by the harshest circumstances or fiercest pressures. Indeed, he seemed to tell us, all the love he had known and all the goodness he wished to bring forth through his own choices were one with what would be lasting, triumphant, and whole.

At times we smile at the idealism of the young, telling ourselves, "They'll learn." At times we fall silent. This fourteen-year-old already understood more about loss than any of the rest of us. He experienced exactly the same pressures and hard choices in life that we did. He also knew his ground. He held to it and lived from it. Confident, with no self-consciousness whatsoever, he offered a vision of wholeness in our midst. Both in his grief and in his choices, he bore among us signs of the greater goodness that he knew would come. After all the years that have passed since that summer, when I think about him I still become silent.

Those who live prophetically act in a manner that honors the root meaning of the word *confidence*. To live with confidence, literally to live with (*cum* in Latin) faith (*fidem*), is to live with trust forever lodged in the One who attends on us all. The elderly woman who raised her eyebrows, the math teacher, and the minister all evinced this confidence. So did the fourteen-year-old I found praying in the church. So have the martyrs of the faith. So, my recollections tell me, did that friend of my family who died so long ago and after whose funeral I first heard the word *integrity*.

I suspect that confidence seldom comes easily to those who live from its power. They do not grasp it in just a moment, or put it on like a shirt or a smile. But through time their confidence grows. It becomes, in each of them, the confidence of the faithful soul who first wrote, "The LORD is my shepherd, I shall not want" (Ps. 23:1). It strengthens into the assurance Jesus pointed to when he said to all his followers, "In the world you face persecution. But take courage; I have conquered the world!" (John 16:33). It widens into the abiding trust Paul offered when in the midst of mounting threats he declared:

> I am convinced that neither death, nor life, nor angels, nor rulers, nor things present, nor things to come, nor powers, nor height, nor depth, nor anything else in all creation, will be able to separate us from the love of God in Christ Jesus our Lord.
>
> —ROMANS 8:38-39

The confidence of those who live prophetically comes from knowing: *God, you are here. You will guide and sustain. However long it takes and whatever hindrances may come, you will make all things whole.*

Here and there across the landscape of our age, such persons shine. They endure at least their share of losses but never let loss speak the final word. With confidence they make courageous choices. When others keep silent, they lament our human brokenness. They urge silence before mystery in a culture that has forgotten how to be still. They cherish simplicity, not in the abstract but in how they clothe themselves and furnish their dwellings, in how they speak and act. They seek justice, not in general but in the daily treatment of the poor, the unemployed, the gay, the person of color, the sojourner from another land. In many of their efforts they meet resistance. In all situations they continue, confident of what ultimately shall be. And both confident and continuing, they offer a form of incarnation. Amid today's crises, they embody the wholeness that in God's time shall come to full flower.

■ ■ ■

FOR PERSONAL MEDITATION

◆ When I think of someone who has lived prophetically, who comes to mind? What did this person do? What did he or she show me?

◆ Where have I lived prophetically? In what ways did I grow from the experience?

◆ What do I find hardest about living prophetically? Is it creating discomfort in other persons? . . . raising difficult questions? . . . enduring opposition? What can help me face these challenges when they arise?

◆ Am I right now being invited to incarnate God's coming wholeness in some area of human need? If so, where?

◆ As a leader, what am I doing to encourage prophetic living in any groups of which I am a part?

◆ As I reflect on the call to live prophetically, for what do I most give thanks?

FOR GROUP REFLECTION

♦ Where do we see the need for prophetic living in our society? . . . in the world? . . . in the church?

♦ When people look at our group, do they perceive prophetic living? When they look at the wider church, where do they see a body of people living prophetically?

♦ What might our group do to encourage prophetic living in the wider bodies and organizations of which we are a part?

♦ What shall we pray for so that we ourselves may more fully bear forth the wholeness that God seeks for us all?

♦ As we reflect on the call to live prophetically, for what do we together give thanks?

The Continuing Invitation

WHENEVER I THINK ON THE WAY OF INTEGRITY, I HEAR AN invitation to come and walk more fully in that way myself.

As I consider the invitation, I am caught by its immediacy. It calls out from work I shall engage in this afternoon. It beckons from the child down the street who needs my compassion and from the friend who needs both my listening and my honest speech. I know the invitation will cry out from any fresh crises I read of on the Internet this evening. Before the day is fully done, the invitation shall, if I allow it, draw me into lamentation, open celebration, or both.

As I consider the invitation, it presents me with no swift answers. Though I yearn for such answers, the way of integrity does not at any point say, "Now here is just the right program to solve this problem, and here is the one to solve that problem." If I move forth in response to the invitation, I shall not find swift answers. I shall, however, find myself drawn into a way of being that will itself become the deepest form of answer.

As I consider the invitation, I see how demanding it is, not only for those who have just started to respond and contemplate going further, but also for those who for years have walked in the way of integrity. Ask them, and they will say that they too are just beginners. Of simplicity? There shall always be more to learn. Endurance? They still seek to grow. Prophetic living? From time to time prophetic living yields changes for the better, but this world will always need prophets. As soon as one harvest of goodness breaks forth, those who live prophetically find themselves pointed toward some new field where once again they must plant for a long while.

The more thoroughly I ponder the invitation, the more I realize it arises from a vast company of persons spread across the ages. They work in fields, homes, schools, laboratories, small shops, offices, and factories. Some preach. Some teach. Some create with their hands. Now and then I glimpse a familiar face among them. A young girl pops up and asks, "Where has all the honesty gone?" A company president continually puts his workers' security ahead of what profits he might glean for himself. An old man labors his way up a seemingly endless flight of stairs leading to a sanctuary, still endures, still presses his way upward into one major cause and then another and then another. He pauses for a moment to catch his breath. He looks around and sees thousands of others doing the same. He nods, then keeps on going. He knows that he and all these others belong together. They are markers in our midst. They move among us as true spiritual leaders. They bear with them the signs and openings for what can make us whole.

And ultimately as I reflect on the invitation, I hear an abiding encouragement from those who offer it. Their encouragement carries not a hint of naïveté, because they have paid dearly for their way of living. Indeed, their steadiness in the face of great cost makes the encouragement all the stronger.

Humbly and with much assurance they say, "Come now. Ground your life in the One who has sustained us and who always will, and you too can walk in this way."

And their words arch out. They beckon. They pull.

Notes

CHAPTER 1

1. William Strauss and Neil Howe, *The Fourth Turning: An American Prophecy* (New York: Broadway Books, 1997), 272. The authors describe a recurrent historical pattern consisting of four movements or "turnings": (1) a High, after society has overcome major adversity; (2) an Awakening, when persons discover that major issues still need to be addressed; (3) an Unraveling, when social bonds decay and society fractures into smaller and smaller groups; and (4) a Crisis, or Fourth Turning, when society is shaken to the core. Strauss and Howe see the last Crisis as encompassing the Great Depression and World War II, the High as running from 1946 to 1964, and the Awakening from 1964 to 1984. The Unraveling they date from 1984. For a full historic profile, readers may wish particularly to explore "Overview: Seven Cycles of Generations and Turnings," 121–38.

2. *The World Almanac and Book of Facts—2002* (New York: World Almanac Education Group, 2002), 870.

3. Joseph B. Verrengia, "Earth Summit Organizers Face Difficult

Task," Associated Press, report from the World Summit for Sustainable Development, *Kalamazoo Gazette*, August 25, 2002.

4. *Statistical Abstract of the United States: 2002*, 122nd ed. (Washington, D.C.: U.S. Census Bureau, 2001), table no. 659, p. 437. In 1980 the lowest fifth of the U.S. population received 5.3 percent of aggregate income; the top 5 percent of the population received 14.6 percent. In 2000 the lowest fifth of the population received 4.3 percent of aggregate income; the top 5 percent of the population received 20.8 percent.

5. John Milton, "Lycidas," line 125, in *John Milton: Paradise Regained, the Minor Poems and Samson Agonistes*, ed. Merritt Y. Hughes (New York: Odyssey Press, 1937), 292.

CHAPTER 2

1. Resources for examination of *integrity* in English, Latin, Hebrew, and Greek are: J. A. Simpson and E. S. C. Weiner, *The Oxford English Dictionary*, 2nd ed. (Oxford: Oxford University Press, 1989); D. P. Simpson, *Cassell's Latin Dictionary* (New York: Macmillan Publishing Co., 1968); *A Hebrew and English Lexicon of the Old Testament*, ed. Francis Brown (Oxford: Oxford University Press, 1962); William F. Arndt and F. Wilbur Gingrich, *A Greek-English Lexicon of the New Testament and Other Early Christian Literature* (Chicago: University of Chicago Press, 1957).

2. For a brief but clear delineation of the relational nature of integrity in the Hebrew scriptures, see the article on "Integrity" by V. H. Kooy in *The Interpreter's Dictionary of the Bible*, vol. 2 (New York: Abingdon Press, 1962), 718.

3. From the first question and answer of The Shorter Catechism adopted by the Westminster Assembly in 1647; *The Constitution of the Presbyterian Church (USA): Part I, Book of Confessions* (Louisville, Ky.: Office of the General Assembly, Presbyterian Church, USA, 1994), 181.

4. Ignatius of Loyola in *Pocket Book of Prayers*, M. Basil Pennington, comp. (New York: Image Books, 1986), 122.

5. Dietrich Bonhoeffer, *Prisoner for God: Letters and Papers from Prison*, ed. Eberhard Bethge and trans. Reginald H. Fuller (New York: Macmillan Company, 1953), 15–16.

CHAPTER 3

1. Harvey L. Rich with Teresa H. Barker, *In the Moment: Celebrating the Everyday* (New York: HarperCollins Publishers, 2002), 154.

2. Terry Tempest Williams, *Leap* (New York: Pantheon Books, 2000), 88.

3. Gerald G. May, M.D., *Will and Spirit: A Contemplative Psychology* (San Francisco: Harper & Row Publishers, 1982), 35.

CHAPTER 5

1. The passages referred to are Matthew 5:37; Luke 23:34; Luke 20:25 (RSV); Matthew 6:7; Matthew 13:33, 38, 44, 46.

CHAPTER 6

1. Calvin W. Laufer in *The Hymnbook* (Richmond, Philadelphia, Pittsburgh, New York: Presbyterian Church in the United States, Presbyterian Church in the United States of America, United Presbyterian Church of North America, Reformed Church in America, 1955), no. 294.

CHAPTER 8

1. This prayer appears in the *Book of Common Worship: Daily Prayer* (Louisville, Ky.: Westminster/John Knox Press, 1993), 39, no. 445. It is originally from *A New Zealand Prayer Book: He Karakia Mihinare o Aotearoa* and is used with permission of the Anglican Church in Aotearoa, New Zealand, and Polynesia.

2. Bonhoeffer, *Prisoner for God*, 86.

CHAPTER 9

1. Edwin H. Friedman, *A Failure of Nerve: Leadership in the*

Age of the Quick Fix, ed. Edward W. Beal and Margaret M. Treadwell (Bethesda, Md.: Edwin Friedman Estate, 1999), 75, 109–16.

Chapter 10

1. Douglas V. Steere, *On Beginning from Within, On Listening to Another* (New York: Harper & Row Publishers, 1964). On the matter of beginning from within, see particularly pp. 43–45 on "The Saint and the Personal Revolution."

About the Author

Steve Doughty, an ordained minister of the Presbyterian Church (USA), has served for twenty-three years as pastor to congregations and ten years as a regional denominational executive. A graduate of the two-year program in spiritual guidance offered by the Shalem Institute for Spiritual Formation, he is the author of three previously published books and numerous essays, and he frequently leads retreats and conferences.

Doughty holds two degrees from Yale University Divinity School and a B.A. degree from Williams College. He and his wife, Jean, live in Otsego, Michigan.

EVERY DAY
Find a Way

Join with Christians around the world who read and pray—every day.

The Upper Room is a daily devotional guide that unites nearly three million Christians around the world into a global Christian community.

If you are searching for ways to deepen your relationship with God, *The Upper Room* is the ideal devotional guide. It encourages Bible reading, prayer, and meditation—practices that help you grow in the faith. Each day's devotion offers a Bible verse, suggested Bible reading, prayer, prayer focus, and thought for the day. Plus, there's a discussion guide for small groups to use. It's the most versatile, economical resource available for church groups or daily devotional practice.

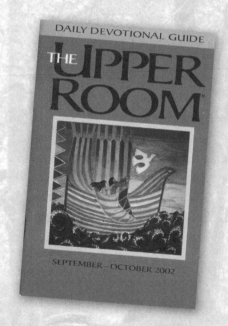

DAILY DEVOTIONAL GUIDE

THE UPPER ROOM

SEPTEMBER – OCTOBER 2002

To order individual
subscriptions, call
1-800-925-6847

To order standing
orders for groups, call
1-800-972-0433

Visit us online today!
www.upperroom.org

Don't Miss These Upper Room Books

Discovering Community
A Meditation on Community in Christ
by Steve Doughty

As an experiment, the author kept a weekly appointment with his journal to answer one question: "Where this past week have I actually seen Christian community?" This book is a sharing of Doughty's discoveries. He looks at community through a number of lenses, focusing on diverse ways and places in which community grows. Prayerful exercises in each chapter, designed for personal and group reflection, invite readers to consider their own sense of community.
ISBN 0-8358-0870-X • 176 pages

Spiritual Preparation for Christian Leadership
by E. Glenn Hinson

In this book, Hinson presents a vision of "living saints" as the model of spiritual leadership for the church. This vision is not about extraordinary or perfect persons but leaders who are "saints" because they have experienced God's grace in their lives and are willing to yield themselves to God.
ISBN 0-8358-0888-2 • 208 pages

The Art of Spiritual Direction
Giving and Receiving Spiritual Guidance
by W. Paul Jones

Writing for clergy and laypersons, W. Paul Jones provides a comprehensive resource on Christian spiritual direction. Drawing on years of experience in receiving and giving spiritual direction, the author helps readers understand the various types of spiritual direction, as well as providing guidelines, methods, and resources for sessions.

ISBN 0-8358-0983-8 • 302 pages

Jesus, Our Spiritual Director
A Pilgrimage through the Gospels
by Wendy J. Miller

In *Jesus, Our Spiritual Director* the reader encounters Jesus as personal spiritual guide and learns how to encourage others in their sacred journey through life. Demonstrating the deep biblical roots of Christian spiritual direction, Wendy Miller brings the Gospel texts to life as a continuing conversation between Jesus and his disciples then and now.

This book is designed for personal reflection and small-group sharing. Church leaders and committed disciples will appreciate Miller's invitation to a more profound relationship with Christ and others on the journey of Christian ministry in the world today.

ISBN 0-8358-9876-8 • 208 pages